Divorce
in New York

The Legal Process,
Your Rights, and What to Expect

Michael D. Stutman, Esq.

Partner and Head of Family Law Group
Mishcon de Reya New York LLP

Addicus Books
Omaha, Nebraska

An Addicus Nonfiction Book

ISBN 978-1-938803-72-7
Typography by Jack Kusler

This book is not intended to serve as a substitute for an attorney. Nor is it the author's intent to give legal advice contrary to that of an attorney. The information contained in this book is for general informational purposes only and should not be relied upon or considered legal advice applicable to a specific legal matter.

Library of Congress Cataloging-in-Publication Data
Stutman, Michael, author.
  Divorce in New York : the legal process, your rights, and what to expect / Michael Stutman.
      p. cm.
  Includes bibliographical references and index.
  ISBN 978-1-938803-72-7 (pbk.)
  1. Divorce--Law and legislation--New York (State) I. Title.
  KFN5126.S78 2013
  346.74701'66--dc23
                                                    2013037578

Addicus Books, Inc.
P.O. Box 45327
Omaha, Nebraska 68145
www.AddicusBooks.com

Printed in the United States of America
10 9 8 7 6 5 4 3 2 1

To all of the Fellows of the American Academy of Matrimonial
Lawyers of the New York Chapter—past, present, and future—
who work tirelessly in pursuit of the Academy credo:

"To preserve the best interests of the Family and of Society,
improve the practice, elevate the standards, advance the cause
of Matrimonial Law."

Contents

Acknowledgments

This book would not have been possible without the contributions of so many people during the more than thirty-five years I have practiced. Although I can't acknowledge you all, I do want to mention several. I acknowledge my good friend and mentor and coauthor of our earlier book, *How to Divorce in New York*, Grier Raggio, who has been a guiding force as long as I can remember. I also gratefully acknowledge my partners at Mishcon de Reya, who believe in this book's message and provide a platform from which it is sent.

Finally, and most importantly, I thank Dana, my wife, a seasoned, talented, and wise matrimonial lawyer in her own right; she has provided the ongoing support and objective insight that is vital to this book project.

Introduction

You've picked up this book because you, or a friend, or a loved one is in crisis—facing a divorce. It seems as though a family is in jeopardy. Dreams may have become nightmares and the future has no structure. It can all be so confusing.

I hope that this book will give you a clear and basic understanding of the legal process that awaits as you go through a divorce. I believe that this clarity will assist you as you make decisions, define your intentions, and set your goals for your future.

1

Understanding the Divorce Process

At a time when your life can feel like it's in utter chaos, sometimes the smallest bit of predictability can bring a sense of comfort. The outcome of many aspects of your divorce may be unknown, driving up your fear and anxiety. But there is one part of your divorce that does have some measure of predictability, and that is the divorce process itself.

Most divorces proceed in a step-by-step manner. Despite the uniqueness of your divorce, you can generally count on one phase of your divorce following the next. Sometimes just realizing you are completing stages and moving forward with your divorce can reassure you that it won't go on forever.

It's important for you to develop a basic understanding of the divorce process. This will lower your anxiety when your attorney starts talking about "depositions" or "going to trial" and you feel your heart start pounding in fear. A basic understanding can reduce your frustration about the length of the process because you understand why each step is needed. This knowledge will support you to begin preparing for what comes next.

Most importantly, understanding the divorce process will make your experience of the entire divorce easier.

1.1   Must I have an attorney to get a divorce in New York?

You are not required to have an attorney to obtain a divorce in New York. However, if your case involves children, maintenance, significant property, or debts, you should avoid proceeding on your own. Life in New York can be a complicated

1

web of legal relationships with landlords, employers, insurance companies, creditors, and, of course, taxes. A lawyer practicing in New York will be able to help you navigate these waters.

If your divorce doesn't involve any of these issues, you can contact your county bar association, which may have clinics for the self-represented and which can provide documents and instructions that are helpful in the simplest of divorce cases. A person who proceeds in a legal matter without a lawyer is referred to as being *pro se* (pronounced pro-say).

If you are considering proceeding without an attorney, at a minimum have an initial consultation with an attorney to discuss your rights and duties under the law. You may have certain rights or obligations about which you are unaware. Meeting with a lawyer can help you decide whether to proceed on your own.

1.2   What is my first step?

If you decide to use an attorney, how do you find a lawyer who is right for you? The choice of an attorney is necessarily intertwined with another judgment you must make: Do you want to try for a mediated or negotiated settlement without going to court? If you believe that you and your spouse are capable of negotiating a settlement either directly between yourselves or through your attorneys, then your attorney should have negotiating skills and the knowledge of New York divorce law and applicable tax law needed to draft a technically sound agreement. The lawyer's litigation experience and ability are less important. However, if you believe that a "war" will be necessary to get satisfactory results with your spouse, or if your spouse has already hired a "bomber" as his or her attorney, then you may need a good courtroom lawyer to protect your interests effectively.

Choosing an Attorney

Before you select a lawyer you must assess your expectations of the attorney-client relationship. After all, you are buying into a highly personal, although temporary, partnership where mutual confidence is a key consideration. This relationship is highly individualized, so it is worth looking around before deciding on the attorney you will hire. Some lawyers can quickly

2

make a client feel secure and comfortable. Others may not be as personable but may be extremely experienced and imaginative in looking for solutions to your particular problems.

Do you expect the attorney to help you decide whether to divorce, or to act as a marriage counselor? If so, you probably are making a mistake. Most lawyers are not qualified to aid you in this way unless they also are trained as marital therapists. Lawyers tend to be concerned primarily with getting the legal process started, documenting your financial situation, readying forms for filing, and developing effective strategies. These are the tasks they have been trained to do.

Look for a lawyer whose practice is involved principally with marital dissolution work. A lawyer's fine reputation in immigration law, for example, is largely irrelevant to your needs. Ask if your potential attorney has been an active member of family law committees in local, state, or national bar associations or is a member of the American Academy of Matrimonial Lawyers, a group that admits only attorneys primarily working in family law. Also, make certain your divorce lawyer has experience with the courts and the legal community in your area. But your own gut reaction, after you have gathered the necessary facts about the lawyer, is your most important guide in finding the right attorney for you.

Reputation and Recommendations: Key Questions

Most people choose lawyers through their reputations or by asking for recommendations from persons whose opinions they value. Divorced friends are a good source of information, particularly if their cases were resolved satisfactorily. Use caution, however, and evaluate your friend's lavish praise (or angry denunciation, for that matter). Inquire closely about those qualities that your friend either admired or disliked in the attorney. You may want to ask some of the following questions:

- Did the attorney's efforts interfere with or facilitate your friend's relations with the former spouse and their children?
- Did your friend feel personally secure and comfortable with the attorney?

3

- Did your friend come away from the process feeling informed?
- Did your friend feel that the attorney's fees and the results of the divorce trial or settlement were fair?

If you follow this route, be sure to see the lawyer to whom you were referred, not his or her associate or partner. Remember that you may want to interview several lawyers before deciding on one who suits you. This is your right. You are the "employer," and in such a critical matter as divorce it is essential that you find an attorney with whom you can communicate and in whom you can place your trust.

If you are referred to a lawyer who is a stranger to you, you can sometimes get background information about the lawyer by consulting reputable directories such as *Martindale-Hubbell and Best Lawyers in America.*

The Initial Conference: A Checklist

During the initial conference you should ask the lawyer questions as well as give information. You need information to determine whether this attorney should handle your case. Your basic standard for choosing will be your own gut reaction to the lawyer personally and as a professional, but answers to the following questions may assist you in formulating or reinforcing that reaction.

What are the attorney's credentials?

Having attended a well-known law school is no guarantee of outstanding ability; however, it helps to know the lawyer's academic background.

- Does the lawyer belong to the city or county bar association? This may indicate respect among peers and suggest respect among the local judges.
- You can check to see on which sections or committees of the bar association the lawyer has served. If he or she has served on sections or committees related to family law, such as the family law sections or the taxation section, or if the lawyer is a member of the

4

American Academy of Matrimonial Lawyers, chances are you're dealing with one of the more committed lawyers in your area.

- Does your lawyer appear on panels or lectures sponsored by law-related organizations? This can also be an indicator of respect among peers and judges.

What portion of the lawyer's time is spent in family law matters?

Many lawyers, particularly in the New York City area and in other major cities, now deal almost exclusively in divorce cases.

Is the lawyer willing to discuss the attitudes of local judges concerning issues relevant to your case?

This would be a good time to discuss general strategies for your case. Again, the relationship between client and lawyer is similar to that of "employer" and "employee." You are the employer, and you have an absolute right to fire your attorney at any time, even without cause. Note, however, that when you change lawyers you will duplicate some of your expenses up to that date because your new attorney will have to become familiar with the facts of your case, and you will likely have to pay for the time this will take.

Communicating with Your Attorney

There are a number of responsibilities that you as a client should observe and certain realities you must recognize if the lawyer is to be as effective and as efficient an advocate as he or she can be:

- Realize that your lawyer cannot guarantee results. Although the lawyer can, and probably will, make predictions about the outcome of your case, the actual outcome of negotiations or litigation may turn on very complex factors.
- Always keep your lawyer informed of any new developments that might affect your cause.
- Take your lawyer's advice, or get another lawyer. You are wasting your money and the lawyer's time if you do not have confidence in the lawyer's special knowledge and skills.

5

- Be utterly candid with your lawyer; tell the truth. Legal advice is worthless if based on faulty or partial information. Tell your lawyer every fact that is relevant to the situation, being careful to include all facts that do *not* appear to be in your favor. Lawyers can plan effective strategies around adverse facts, but only if they are aware of them.

1.3 What information should I take with me to the first meeting with my attorney?

Attorneys differ on the amount of information they like to see at an initial consultation. When you make the initial appointment, ask what documents the attorney would like to see. If a court proceeding, either a divorce or a proceeding where an order of protection is being sought, has already been initiated by either you or your spouse, it is important to bring copies of any court documents.

If you have a prenuptial or postnuptial agreement with your spouse, that is another important document for you to bring at the outset of your case.

If you intend to ask for support, either for yourself or for children, documents evidencing income of both you and your spouse will also be useful. These might include:

- Recent pay stubs
- Individual and business tax returns, W-2s, and 1099s
- Bank statements showing deposits
- A recent loan application
- A statement of your monthly budget

Your attorney may ask you to complete a questionnaire at the time of your first meeting. When you schedule your first meeting, ask if a questionnaire will be completed. If so, ask whether it is possible to do this in advance of your meeting. This can allow you to provide more complete information and to make the most of your appointment time with the lawyer.

If your situation is urgent or you do not have access to these documents, don't let it stop you from scheduling your appointment with an attorney. In the beginning, prompt legal advice about your rights is often more important than having detailed financial information. Your attorney can explain to you the options for obtaining these financial records if they are not readily available to you.

1.4   What unfamiliar words might an attorney use at the first meeting?

Law has a language all its own, and attorneys sometimes lapse into "legalese," forgetting that nonlawyers may not recognize words used daily in the practice of law. Some words and phrases you might hear include:

Dissolution of marriage—The divorce

Plaintiff—Person who starts the legal process

Defendant—Person who did not start the legal process

Jurisdiction—Authority of a court to make rulings affecting a party

Service—Process of notifying a party about a legal filing

Discovery—Process during which each side provides information to the other

Divorce decree—The final order entered in a divorce

Never hesitate to ask your attorney the meaning of a term. Your complete understanding of your lawyer's advice is essential for you to partner with your advocate as effectively as possible.

Even if you are not yet ready to start a process for divorce, call to schedule an appointment to obtain information about protecting yourself and your children. Even if you are not planning to file for divorce soon, your spouse might be.

1.5   Is New York a *no-fault* state or do I need grounds for a divorce?

In October of 2010, New York became a *no-fault* divorce state. This means that for divorce cases that began after October of 2010, neither you nor your spouse is required to prove that the other is "at fault" in order to be granted a divorce. Factors such as infidelity, cruelty, or abandonment are not necessary to receive a divorce in New York. Rather, it is necessary to prove only that the marriage is "irretrievably broken" to have it dissolved.

The testimony of either you or your spouse is likely to be sufficient evidence for the court to rule that the marriage should be dissolved. This testimony, usually given by the spouse who filed for the divorce, will state that the marriage is irretrievably broken and was so broken for more than six months before the divorce proceeding was begun.

1.6   Do I have to get divorced in the same state I married in?

No. Regardless of where you were married, you may seek a divorce in New York if the jurisdictional requirements of residency are met.

1.7   How long do I have to have lived in New York to get a divorce in the state?

Either you or your spouse must meet certain residency requirements depending on the circumstances. For example, if you were married in New York, one of you needs to be a resident for a year before starting the divorce. Or, if the two of you had a residence in the state as husband and wife at any time and one of you had been a resident for a year before starting to divorce, you are eligible to obtain a divorce in New York. You are also eligible if either of you had been a resident for two years before starting the action. There is one section providing that if you reside in New York when "the cause of action" arises you can file at that time.

If neither party meets the residency requirement, other legal options are available for your protection. If you do not meet the one-year residency requirement, talk to your attorney about options such as a legal separation, a petition for custody and support order, or a protection order.

1.8   My spouse has told me she will never "give me" a divorce. Can I get one in New York anyway?

Yes. New York does not require that your spouse "agree to" a divorce. If your spouse threatens to "not give you a divorce," know that in New York this is an idle threat without any basis in the law.

Under New York law, to obtain a divorce you must be able to prove only that your marriage is "irretrievably broken." Evidence of this will be your testimony on the witness stand.

In short, it is not necessary to have your spouse agree to the divorce or to allege the specific difficulties that arose during the marriage to obtain a divorce in New York.

The Divorce Process Initiated by Litigation
Obtain a referral for a lawyer.
Schedule an appointment with an attorney.
Prepare questions and gather needed documents for initial consultation.
Meet for initial consultation with attorney.
Sign retainer agreement.
Provide requested information and documents to your attorney.
Take other actions as advised by attorney, such as opening or closing financial accounts.
Attorney prepares summons, and perhaps, complaint for divorce, net worth statement, temporary maintenance calculations, and affidavits for temporary matters for your review and signature.
Attorney files summons, and perhaps, complaint with county clerk. Automatic *ex parte* restraints become effective against you.
Attorney obtains court date for interim matters and preliminary conference if necessary. In New York, the interim order is known as a *pendente lite* order.
Spouse is served summons, complaint, notice of automatic restraints, and any motion papers.
Negotiations begin regarding terms of the *pendente lite* order on matters such as custody, support, and temporary possession of the family home.
Parties appear for motion argument and preliminary conference. Parties complete preliminary conference order.
If the terms of the *pendente lite* order are reached by agreement, the parties prepare a stipulation that is then "so ordered" by the court. If the parties don't agree, the papers are all submitted to a judge, who is supposed to issue a decision within sixty days.
If there are minor children, parties comply with any local rules or court orders to attend parent education class, develop a parenting plan, or participate in mediation.
Both sides conduct discovery to obtain information regarding all relevant facts.
Obtain valuations of assets, including expert opinions if needed.
Confer with attorney to review facts, identify issues, assess strengths and weaknesses of the case, review strategy, and develop proposal for settlement.

The Divorce Process Initiated by Litigation
Spouses with support of attorneys attempt to reach agreement through written proposals, mediation, settlement conferences, or other negotiation.
Parties reach agreement on all issues.
Attorneys prepare settlement agreement, judgment of divorce, and relevant court orders for the division of retirement plans for approval by spouses and attorneys.
OR
Note of Issue and Certificate of Readiness for trial is filed with the court asking that a court date be set.
Parties prepare for trial on unresolved issues, including: preparation of witnesses, trial exhibits, legal research on contested issues, pretrial motions, trial brief, preparation of direct and cross-examination of witnesses, preparation of opening statement, subpoena of witnesses, closing argument, and suggestions to the court.
Meet with attorney for final trial preparation
Trial (May go day-to-day or spread out over a number of weeks or months)
Judge makes decision.
Attorney prepares judgment. Spouse's attorney approves it as to form or submits "counter" prepared judgment. Prepared judgment(s) submitted to judge for signature.
Make payments and sign documents (deeds or titles) pursuant to the judgment.

1.9   Can I divorce my spouse in New York if he or she lives in another state?

Provided you have met the residency requirements for living in New York, you can file for divorce in the state even if your spouse lives in another state.

Discuss with your attorney the facts that will need to be proven and the steps necessary to give your spouse proper notice to ensure that the court will have jurisdiction over your spouse. Your attorney can counsel you on whether it is possible to proceed with the divorce. Under certain circumstances, you might only be able to obtain a divorce, that is a decree ending the marriage, but not necessarily distributing property; determining support for you, your spouse, or your children; or determining child custody. A simple divorce will cut off your right to inherit a share of your spouse's estate (and vice versa), it will change your tax filing status, it will impact health insurance, and it may affect certain personal retirement plan rights and eligibility.

1.10 How can I divorce my spouse when I don't know where this person lives now?

New York law allows you to proceed with a divorce even if you do not know the current address of your spouse. In order to have a court authorize the use of a procedure that does not require the actual delivery to your spouse of the divorce summons, you need to satisfy certain requirements.

First, take action to attempt to locate your spouse. Contact family members, friends, former coworkers, or anyone else who might know your spouse's whereabouts.

Utilize resources on the Internet that are designed to help locate people. To the extent you can prove you made these efforts, collect such proof.

Let your attorney know of the efforts you have made to attempt to find your spouse. Inform your lawyer of your spouse's last known address, as well as any work address or other address where this person may be found. Once your attorney attempts to give notice to your spouse without success, it is possible to ask the court to proceed with the divorce by giving notice through publication in a newspaper.

Although your divorce may be granted following service of notice by publication in a newspaper, you may not be able to get other court orders such as those for child support or alimony without giving personal notice to your spouse. Talk to your attorney about your options and rights if you don't know where your spouse is living.

1.11 I just moved to a different county within New York. Must I file in the county where my spouse lives?

You may file your divorce summons and complaint in any county in the State of New York. If your spouse objects to the county you selected, your spouse may initiate a process to require that you change the county to one that your spouse deems more appropriate. Generally, if you file in the county of your residence, your spouse's residence, or where you and your spouse have a joint residence, your spouse will be hard-pressed to change it. The selection of the county can be important depending on the location of witnesses, convenience, or the law applied. Although New York has its own state laws, the state is divided into four judicial departments and each department has its own subtle nuances in its interpretation of the law.

1.12   I immigrated to New York. Will my immigration status stop me from getting a divorce?

If you meet the residency requirements for divorce in New York, you can get a divorce here notwithstanding your immigration status. Talk to your immigration lawyer about the likelihood of a divorce leading to immigration challenges.

If you are a victim of domestic violence, tell your lawyer. You may be eligible for a change in your immigration status under federal law.

1.13   I want to get divorced in my Indian tribal court. What do I need to know?

Each Indian tribal court has its own laws governing divorce. Requirements for residency, grounds for divorce, and the laws regarding property, alimony, and children can vary substantially from state law. Some tribes have very different laws governing the grounds for your divorce, removal of children from the home, and cohabitation.

Contact an attorney who is knowledgeable about the law in your tribal court for legal advice on pursuing a divorce in your tribal court or on the requirements for recording a divorce obtained in a state court with the clerk of the tribal court.

1.14   Is there a waiting period for a divorce in New York?

No.

1.15   What is a divorce *complaint?*

A divorce *complaint,* also referred to as a *verified complaint for divorce,* is a document signed by the person filing for divorce and filed with the clerk of the court at the entry point of the divorce process. The complaint will set forth in very general terms the basis for divorce, facts that give the court jurisdiction and statements regarding what the plaintiff is asking the court to order.

The New York State Unified Court System has created certain standard forms regarding a wide range of circumstances that may surface in your case. You can find these forms at www.nycourts.gov/divorce/ along with other information.

1.16 My spouse said she filed for divorce last week, but there's nothing on file at the courthouse. What does it mean to "file for divorce"?

When lawyers use the term *filing* they are ordinarily referring to filing a legal document at the courthouse, such as delivering a summons and complaint or summons with notice for divorce to the clerk of the court with the proper filing fee. Sometimes a person who has hired a lawyer to begin a divorce action uses the phrase "I've filed for divorce," although no papers have yet been taken to the courthouse to start the legal process.

1.17 If we both want a divorce, does it matter who files?

It depends. In the eyes of the court, the plaintiff (the party who files the complaint initiating the legal process of the divorce) and the defendant (the other spouse) are not seen differently by virtue of which party filed.

Your attorney may advise you to file first or to wait until your spouse files, depending upon the overall strategy for your case and your circumstances. For example, if there is a concern that your spouse will begin to transfer assets upon learning about your plans for divorce, your attorney might advise you to file immediately to trigger the "automatic orders." These are orders intended to maintain the "status quo." These orders are more fully explained in chapter 7, question 7.9. Further, if you and your spouse have more than one residence, your attorney may advise you to file to lock in your choice of the county. Further, the plaintiff often has the burden of proof on certain issues and the defendant has priority in discovery, so you may want to wait for your spouse to file. If you are separated from your spouse but have a beneficial temporary arrangement, your attorney may counsel you to wait for your spouse to file. As you see, it is a complicated decision.

Allow your attorney to support you in making the decision about whether, when, and where to initiate the legal process by filing.

1.18   Will the filing for divorce be public knowledge?

Most documents filed in divorce are not open for public inspection. However, the fact that a divorce has begun can be determined if someone wants to look into the matter.

1.19   Is there a way to avoid embarrassing my spouse and not have him served with the divorce papers where others might see (like the workplace)?

Talk to your lawyer about the option of having your spouse and his lawyer sign a document that acknowledges the service of the papers. The signing and filing of this document with the court can eliminate the need to have your spouse served by a third party.

1.20   Should I sign an acknowledgment of service of divorce papers even if I don't agree with what my spouse has written in the complaint for divorce?

There may be some reasons to insist on the formality of personal service, but signing the acknowledgment does not mean that you agree with anything your spouse has stated in the divorce complaint or anything that your spouse is asking for in the divorce.

Signing the acknowledgment only substitutes for having a third party personally hand you the documents. You do not waive the right to object to anything your spouse has stated in the complaint.

Follow your attorney's advice on whether and when to sign a voluntary acknowledgment.

1.21   Why should I contact an attorney right away if I have received divorce papers?

If your spouse has filed for divorce, the filing itself has immediately changed your legal relationship with your spouse and it is important that you obtain legal advice as soon as possible so that you understand what is occurring. Even if you and your spouse are getting along, having independent legal counsel can help you make decisions now that could affect your divorce later.

After your spouse has filed for divorce, certain automatic orders are triggered. Time periods for certain actions on your part have been established, and perhaps court appearances will be scheduled. It is possible you will not receive much advance notice of the first court appearance, yet you need to spend adequate time selecting your attorney and preparing for a court appearance.

After you receive the *summons with notice* or *summons and complaint* (whether you have acknowledged receipt or have been served by a third party), a written appearance must be filed with the court within twenty days (assuming you were served in New York State).

1.22   What is an *ex parte* court order?

An *ex parte* court order is obtained when one party (in this case you or your spouse) goes to a judge to ask for something without giving prior notice or giving the other side an opportunity to be heard.

With the exception of order of protection, judges are reluctant to sign *ex parte* orders. Ordinarily, the court will require the other side to have notice of any requests for court orders, and an appearance before the judge will be held.

When an *ex parte* order is granted, the court ordinarily sets a date for an appearance soon thereafter so that the party who did not request the order has an opportunity to tell his or her side of the story and have the judge determine whether the order should remain in effect.

1.23   What is a motion?

A *motion* is a request that the judge enter an order of some type. For example, your attorney may file a written motion with the court asking for temporary custody and child support.

Some motions are made to handle certain procedural aspects of your case, such as a motion to seek a party's compliance with requests for documents or other information. In many courts, procedural matters that are more administrative in nature (like scheduling matters) are handled via a conference call with the judge or someone in the judge's chambers.

1.24 Once my complaint for divorce is filed, how long will it take before a preliminary conference is held?

In most cases a preliminary conference will be held within forty-five days of a request being filed with the court, assuming your spouse can be located to be given notice. A preliminary conference is a meeting in the courthouse with both parties, their attorneys, and the judge. The purpose of the meeting is to establish what aspects of your case are in dispute, what is not in dispute, what experts may be needed, how some expenses are paid, and so on. Also, a schedule for your case is created. The preliminary conference form may be found at www.courts.state.ny.us/forms/matrimonial/preliminaryconference.pdf.

1.25 How much notice will I get if my spouse seeks a motion for a *pendente lite* order?

New York law requires that you receive "reasonable notice" of any court hearings. Depending on the circumstances, this notice may be very short. A *pendente lite* order is an order that directs the parties to do certain things until the trial. It can cover things such as support, child access, attorney fees, use of home, and payment of expenses.

1.26 During my divorce, what am I responsible for doing?

Your attorney will explain what actions you should take to further the divorce process and to help you reach the best possible outcome.

You will be asked to:

- Keep in regular contact with your attorney.

- Update your attorney regarding any changes in your contact information, such as address, phone numbers, and e-mail address.

- Provide your attorney with all requested documents or authorizations so that the documents can be obtained from others (like banks, insurance companies, health care providers, employers, etc.).

- Provide requested information in a timely manner.

- Complete forms and questionnaires.

- Appear in court on time.
- Be direct about asking any questions you might have.
- Tell your attorney your thoughts on settlement or what you would like the judge to order in your case.
- Remain respectful toward your spouse throughout the process.
- Comply with any temporary court orders, such as restraining or support orders.
- Advise your attorney of any significant developments in your case.

By doing your part in the divorce process, you enable your attorney to partner with you for a better outcome while also lowering your attorney fees.

1.28 My spouse has all of our financial information. How will I be able to prepare for negotiations and trial if I don't know the facts or have the documents?

Once your divorce has been filed with the court and a preliminary conference has been held, your attorney will proceed to obtain documents and other information needed to prepare your case for a settlement or trial, within the time periods established at the preliminary conference.

1.27 I'm worried that I won't remember to ask my lawyer about all of the issues in my case. How can I be sure I don't miss anything?

Write down all of the topics you want to discuss with your attorney, including what your goals are for the outcome of the divorce. The sooner you clarify your goals, the easier it will be for your attorney to advise you as to how realistic your goals are and what the cost of pursuing them might be. Realize that your attorney will think of some issues that you may not have thought of. Your lawyer's experience will be helpful in making sure nothing important is forgotten. On the two pages that follow is a divorce issues checklist summarizing common issues in New York divorce cases:

Divorce Issues Checklist

	Notes
Dissolution of marriage	
Prenuptial agreements	
Postnuptial agreements	
Custody of minor children	
Removal of children from jurisdiction	
Parenting plan (time, transportation, etc.)	
Child support	
Extraordinary expenses warranting a deviation in child support	
Summer child support abatement	
Life insurance to fund unpaid child support	
Automatic withholding for support	
Child-care expenses	
Health insurance for minor children	
Uninsured medical expenses for minor children	
Private school tuition for children	
College expenses for children	
Health insurance for the parties	
Real property: marital residence (deed, refinancing, sale)	
Real property: rentals, cabins, commercial property, etc. (deed, refinancing, sale)	
Marital expenses associated with real estate	
Time shares	
Retirement plans (401k, Simple IRA, TSA, etc.), possible QDROs	
Federal or military pensions	
Businesses	

Divorce Issues Checklist

Enhanced earning capacity	
Bank accounts	
Investments	
Stock options	
Premarital or nonmarital assets	
Premarital or nonmarital debts	
Pets	
Personal property division including: motor vehicles, recreational vehicles, campers, airplanes, collections, furniture, electronics, tools, household goods, etc.	
Exchange date for personal property	
Division of marital debt	
Property settlement	
Maintenance	
Life insurance to fund unpaid maintenance	
Sums owed under production	
Tax exemptions for minor children	
IRS Form 8332 for claiming children as dependents	
Filing status for tax returns for the last/current year	
Restoration of former name	
Attorney fees	

1.29 My spouse and I both want our divorce to be amicable. How can we keep it that way?

You and your spouse are to be commended for your willingness to cooperate while focusing on moving through the divorce process. This will not only make your lives easier and save you money on attorney fees, but it is also more likely to result in an outcome that satisfies you both. I regularly appear before a judge who often tells the parties "The way you end this relationship sets the stage for the next part of your life." If your goal is to reach an amicable resolution, find a lawyer who understands your goal and encourage your spouse to do the same. Cooperate with the prompt exchange of necessary information. Then ask your attorney about the options of mediation and negotiation for reaching agreement. Even if you are not able to settle all of the issues in your divorce, these actions can increase the likelihood of reaching an agreement on many of the terms of your divorce.

1.30 Can I get a different judge?

Talk to your attorney about the reasons you want a different judge. If you believe that your judge has a conflict of interest, such as being a close friend with your spouse, you may have a basis for asking the judge to be "recused" in order to allow another judge to hear the case. Ordinarily, though, you will not be able to choose another judge.

1.31 How long will it take to get my divorce?

The more you and your spouse are in agreement, the faster your divorce will conclude. At a minimum, it takes thirty to sixty days from the date your agreement is signed and the divorce papers are submitted to a court. If you do not reach an agreement on all the issues and require a judge to rule on a contested matter, your divorce could take fourteen months or more.

1.32 What is the significance of my divorce being final?

The finality of your divorce, referred to as the *judgment of divorce*, is important for many reasons. It affects your right to remarry, your rights to inherit from your spouse (and vice versa), your ability to change insurance beneficiaries, your eligibility for health insurance from your former spouse, your filing status for income taxes, and many other obligations.

1.33 When does my divorce become final?

Your divorce becomes final the day the judge signs your judgment of divorce and it is entered in the county clerk's office. Under some circumstances the mere signing of the judgment by the judge will be sufficient.

1.34 Can I start using my former name right away and how do I get my name legally restored?

You may begin using your former name at any time, provided you are not doing so for any unlawful purpose, such as to avoid your creditors. Many agencies and institutions, however, will not alter their records without a court order changing your name. The judgment of divorce will state that you are permitted to resume the use of your former name. If the judgment of divorce does not state this (along with what your former name is), you must then pursue a civil name change proceeding, which is surprisingly expensive.

2

Coping with Stress
during the Divorce Process

It may have been a few years ago. Or, it may have been
many years ago. Perhaps it was only months. But when
you said, "I do," you meant it. Like most people getting married,
you planned to be a happily married couple for life.

But things happen. Life brings change. People change.
Whatever the circumstance, you now find yourself considering
divorce. The emotions of divorce may run from one extreme
to another as you journey through the process. You may feel
relief and are ready to move on with your life. On the other
hand, you may feel emotions that are quite painful: Anger.
Fear. Sorrow. A deep sense of loss or failure. Remember, it
is important to find support for coping with all these strong
emotions.

Because going through a divorce can be an emotional
time, having a clear understanding of the divorce process and
what to expect will help you make better decisions. And when
it comes to decision making, search inside yourself to clarify
your intentions and goals for the future. Let these intentions be
your guide.

During the last thirty-five years I have observed the
strategies some of my clients have used to deal with the
emotional turmoil that a divorce may cause. I thought it might
be helpful if I shared some of my thoughts regarding what I've
seen over the years.

2.1   My spouse left home weeks ago. I don't want a divorce because I feel our marriage can be saved. Should I still see an attorney?

Yes. Whether you want a divorce or not, there are important actions for you to take now to protect your assets, credit, home, children, and future right to support.

2.2   The thought of going to a lawyer's office to talk about divorce is more than I can bear. I canceled the first appointment I made because I just couldn't do it. What should I do?

Many people going through a divorce are dealing with lawyers for the first time and feel anxious about the experience. Ask a trusted friend or family member to go with you. He or she can support you by writing down your questions in advance, by taking notes for you during the meeting, and by helping you to remember what the lawyer said after the meeting is concluded. It is very likely that you will feel greatly relieved just to be better informed.

2.3   There is some information about my marriage that I think my attorney needs, but I'm too embarrassed to discuss it. Must I tell the attorney?

Your attorney has an ethical duty to maintain confidentiality. Past events in your marriage are matters that your lawyer is obligated to keep private. The information you provide your attorney is *privileged.* That means more than *confidential.* Privileged information cannot be disclosed under *any* circumstances. So for example, your attorney could not be forced to disclose the information even if he or she received a subpoena. Confidential information does not have that sort of protection.

Attorneys who practice divorce law are accustomed to hearing a lot of intimate information about families. Although such information is deeply personal to you, it is unlikely that anything you tell your lawyer will be a shock.

Although it may feel uncomfortable for a short moment, it is important that your attorney have complete information so that your interests can be fully protected. If speaking directly about these facts still seems too difficult, consider putting them in a letter.

2.4   I'm unsure about how to tell our children about the divorce, and I'm worried I'll say the wrong thing. What's the best way?

How you talk to your children about the divorce will depend upon their ages and development. It is strongly suggested that you and your spouse coordinate telling your children and you may consider a consultation with a mental health professional for guidance. Changes in your children's everyday lives, such as a change of residence or one parent leaving the home, are the areas of importance to your children. Information about legal proceedings and meetings with lawyers are really not the children's concern and are best kept among adults.

Simpler answers are best for young children. Avoid giving them more information than they need.

You may find that the *initial discussion* is not a discussion at all. It may be more that you tell the children what is going on. It's a big piece of information for children to digest and it will take time for them to do so. Keep the door open for further talks. Create opportunities for them to bring up the subject. Use these times to acknowledge their feelings and offer support.

2.5   My youngest child seems very depressed about the divorce, the middle one is angry, and my teenager is skipping school. How can I cope?

A child's reaction to divorce can vary depending upon his or her age and other factors. Some may cry and beg for reconciliation, and others may act out. Reducing conflict with your spouse, being a consistent and nurturing parent, and making sure both of you remain involved are all actions that can support your children regardless of how they are reacting to the divorce.

Support groups for children whose parents are divorcing are available at many schools and religious communities. A school counselor can also provide support. If more help is needed, confer with a therapist experienced in working with children.

2.6   I am so frustrated by my spouse's "Disneyland parent" behavior. Is there anything I can do to stop this?

Feelings of guilt, competition, or remorse sometimes lead a parent to be tempted to spend parenting time in trips to the toy store and special activities. Other times they can result in an absence of discipline in an effort to become the favored parent or to make the time "special."

Shift your focus from the other parent's behavior to your own, and do your best to be an outstanding parent during this time. Keep routines for your child for family meals, bedtimes, chores, and homework. Encourage family activities, as well as individual time with each child when it's possible.

During a time when a child's life is changing, providing a consistent and stable routine in your home can ease his or her anxiety and provide comfort.

Attempting to buy your child's loyalty with tangible items or special treatments will likely backfire.

2.7   Between requests for information from my spouse's lawyer and my own lawyer, I am totally overwhelmed. How do I manage gathering all of this detailed information by the deadlines imposed?

First, simply get started. An old friend of mine used to tell me that when he was a boy, he worked on a hay truck. He got five cents for each bale he put on the truck. He said if he ever started to count the money as he earned it, he would have quit before he made $1.00 Often, thinking about a task is worse than the job itself.

Second, break it down into smaller tasks. Perhaps one evening you gather your tax returns and on the weekend you work on your monthly living expenses.

Third, let in support. Ask that friend of yours who just loves numbers to come over for an evening with her calculator to help you get organized.

Finally, communicate with your lawyer. Your attorney or paralegal may be able to make your job easier by giving you suggestions or help. It may be that essential information can be provided now and the details submitted later.

2.8   I am so depressed about my divorce that I'm having difficulty getting out of bed in the morning to care for my children. What should I do?

See your health care provider. Feelings of depression are common during a divorce. You also want to make sure that you identify any physical health concerns, too.

Although feelings of sadness are common during a divorce, more serious depression means it's time to seek some professional support.

Your health and your ability to care for your children are both essential. Follow through on recommendations by your health care professionals for therapy, medication, or other measures to improve your wellness.

2.9   I know I need help to cope with the stress of the divorce, but I can't afford counseling. What can I do?

You are wise to recognize that divorce is a time for letting in support. You can explore a number of options, including:

• Meeting with a member of the clergy or lay chaplain

• Joining a divorce support group

• Turning to friends and family members

• Going to a therapist or divorce counselor. If budget is a concern, contact a social agency that offers counseling services on a sliding-fee scale.

If none of these options are available, look again at your budget. You may see that counseling is important enough that you decide to find a way to increase your income or lower your expenses to support this investment in your well-being.

2.10   I'm the one who filed for divorce, but I still have loving feelings toward my spouse and feel sad about divorcing. Does this mean I should dismiss my divorce?

Strong feelings of caring about your spouse often persist after a divorce is filed. Whether or not to proceed with a divorce is a deeply personal decision. Although feelings can inform us of our thoughts, sometimes they can also cause us to not look clearly at everything there is to see in our situation.

Have you and your spouse participated in marriage counseling? Has your spouse refused to seek treatment for an addiction? Are you worried about your safety or that of your children if you remain in the marriage? Can you envision yourself as financially secure if you remain in this marriage? Is your spouse involved in another relationship?

The answer to these questions can help you get clear about whether to consider reconciliation. Talk to your therapist, coach, or spiritual advisor to help determine the right path for you.

2.11 Will my lawyer charge me for the time I spend talking about my feelings about my spouse and my divorce?

Most likely, yes. If you are paying your attorney by the hour, expect to be charged for the time your attorney spends talking with you. If your attorney is being paid a flat rate for handling your divorce, the time spent talking with you will be included in the fee.

2.12 My lawyer doesn't seem to realize how difficult my divorce is for me. How can I get him to understand?

Everyone wants support and compassion from the professionals who are helping them during a divorce. Speak frankly with your attorney about your concerns. It may be that your lawyer does not see your concerns as being relevant to the job of getting your desired outcome in the divorce. Perhaps your lawyer is concerned about using her time efficiently and keeping her charges to you relating only to the work she is trained to do. Your willingness to improve the communication will help your lawyer understand how best to support you in the process and will help you understand which matters are best left for discussion with your therapist or a supportive friend.

2.13 I've been told not to speak ill of my spouse in front of my child, but I know my spouse is doing this all the time. Why can't I just speak the truth?

It can be devastating for your child to hear you badmouthing his or her other parent. What your child needs is permission to love both of you, regardless of any bad parental behavior. The best way to support your child during this time is to encourage a positive relationship with the other parent.

2.14 Nobody in our family has ever been divorced, and I feel really ashamed. Will my children feel the same way?

Making a change in how you see your family identity is huge for you. The best way to help your children is to establish a sense of pride in their new family and to look forward to the future with a real sense of opportunity.

Your children will have an opportunity to witness you overcoming obstacles, demonstrating independence, and moving forward in your life notwithstanding challenges. You can be a great teacher to them during this time by demonstrating pride in your family and in yourself.

2.15 I am terrified of having my deposition taken. My spouse's lawyer is very aggressive, and I'm afraid I'm going to say something that will hurt my case.

A deposition is an opportunity for your spouse's attorney to gather information and to assess the type of witness you will be if the case proceeds to trial. Feeling anxious about your deposition is normal. However, regardless of the personality of the lawyers, most depositions in divorces are quite uneventful.

Remember that your attorney will be seated by your side at all times to support you. Ask to meet with your lawyer in advance to prepare for the deposition. If you are worried about certain questions that might be asked, talk to your attorney about them. Think of it as an opportunity, and enlist your lawyer's support in being well prepared.

2.16 I am still so angry at my spouse, how can I be expected to sit in the same room during a settlement conference?

If you are still really angry at your spouse, it may be beneficial to postpone the conference for a time. You might also consider seeking some counseling to support you with coping with your feelings of anger.

Another option might be *shuttle* negotiations. With this method, you and your attorney remain in one room while your spouse and his or her attorney are in another. Settlement offers are then relayed between the attorneys throughout the negotiation process. By shifting your focus from your angry feelings to your goal of a settlement, it may be easier to proceed through the process.

2.17 I'm afraid I can't make it through court without having an emotional breakdown. How do I prepare?

A divorce trial can be a highly emotional time, calling for lots of support. Your anxiety is certainly a by-product of your sense that this is a process over which you have little understanding or control. So a good way to help yourself is to do what you can to develop a true understanding about what the issues are and what information is important. In this regard you should:

- Meet with your lawyer or the firm's support staff in advance of your court date to prepare you for court.

- Ask your lawyer whether there are any documents you should review in preparation for court, such as your deposition.

- Visit the courtroom in advance to get comfortable with the surroundings.

- Ask your lawyer about having a support person with you on your court date.

- Ask yourself what the worst thing is that could happen and consider what options you would have if it did.

- Avoid alcohol, eat healthfully, exercise, and get plenty of rest during the period of time leading up to the court date. Each of these will help you to prepare for the emotions of the day.

- Plan what you intend to wear in advance. Small preparations will lower your stress.

- Visualize the experience going well. Picture yourself sitting in the witness stand, giving clear, confident, and truthful answers to easy questions.

- Arrive early at the courthouse and make sure you have a plan for parking your car if you are not familiar with the area.

- Take slow, deep breaths. Breathing deeply will steady your voice, calm your nerves, and improve your focus.

Your attorney will be prepared to support you throughout the proceedings. By taking the above steps, you can increase the ease of your experience.

2.18   I am really confused. One day I think I've made a mistake, the next day I know I can't go back, and a few minutes later I can hardly wait to be single again. Some days I just don't believe I'm getting divorced. What's happening?

What you are experiencing is normal for a person going through divorce. Denial, transition, and acceptance are common passages for a person during the divorce process. One moment you might feel excited about your future and a few hours later you think your life is ruined.

What can be helpful to remember is that you may not pass from one stage to the next in a direct line. Feelings of anger or sadness may well up in you long after you thought you had moved on. Similarly, your mood might feel bright one day as you think about your future plans, even though you still miss your spouse.

Taking good care of yourself is essential during this period of your life. What you are going through requires a tremendous amount of energy. Allow yourself to experience your emotions, but also continue moving forward with your life. These steps will help your life get easier day by day.

3

Working with an Attorney

If there is only one thing you can be sure of in your divorce, it's that you will be given plenty of advice. Well-intentioned neighbors, cousins, and complete strangers will be happy to tell you war stories about their ex or about their sister who got divorced in Canada. Many will insist they know what you should do, even though they haven't the vaguest notion of the facts of your case or the law in New York.

But there is one person whose advice will matter to you: your attorney. Your lawyer should be your trusted and supportive advocate at all times throughout your divorce. The counsel of your attorney can affect your life for years to come. You will never regret taking the time and energy to choose the right one for you.

See your relationship with your attorney as a partnership for pursuing what is most important to you. With clear and open attorney-client communication, you'll have the best outcome possible and your entire divorce process will be less stressful. By working closely with the right lawyer, you can trust the professional advice you receive.

3.1   My spouse says because we're still friends we should use the same attorney for the divorce. Is this a good idea?

Even the most amicable of divorcing couples usually have differing interests. For this reason, it is never recommended that an attorney represent both parties in a divorce. In most cases, an attorney is ethically prohibited from representing two people with conflicting interests who are in dispute.

31

Sometimes couples have reached agreements without understanding all of their rights under the law. A client often will benefit from receiving further legal advice on matters such as tax considerations, retirement, and health insurance issues.

It is not uncommon for one party to retain an attorney and for the other party not to do so. In such cases, the party with the attorney files the complaint, and agreements reached between the parties are typically sent to the spouse for approval prior to any court hearing. If your spouse has filed for divorce and said that you do not need an attorney, you should nevertheless meet with a lawyer for advice on how proceeding without a lawyer could affect your legal rights.

3.2   What can I expect at an initial consultation with an attorney?

The nature of the advice you get from an attorney in an initial consultation will depend upon whether you are still deciding whether you want a divorce, whether you are planning for a possible divorce in the future, or whether your are ready to file for divorce right away.

With few exceptions, the information you provide an attorney, whether you ultimately retain that attorney or not, is absolutely privileged.

During the meeting, you will have an opportunity to provide the following information to the attorney:

- A brief history of the marriage
- Background information regarding yourself, your spouse, and your children
- Your immediate situation
- Your intentions and goals regarding your relationship with your spouse
- Your financial circumstances (income from all sources, assets, liabilities, special circumstances)
- What information you are seeking from the attorney during the consultation

Working with an Attorney

You can expect the attorney to provide the following information to you:

- The procedure for divorce in New York
- A preliminary list of the issues important in your case
- A preliminary assessment of your rights and responsibilities under the law
- Background information regarding the firm
- Information about fees and billings

Although some questions may be impossible for the attorney to answer at the initial consultation because additional information or research is needed, the initial consultation is an opportunity for you to ask all of the questions you have at the time of the meeting.

3.3   Can I take a friend or family member to my initial consultation?

Yes. Having someone present during your initial consultation can be a source of great support. You might ask him or her to take notes on your behalf so that you can focus on listening and asking questions. Remember that this is your consultation, however, and it is important that the attorney hear the facts of your case directly from you.

3.4   What exactly will my attorney do to help me get a divorce?

Your attorney will play a critical role in helping you get your divorce. You will be actively involved in some of the work, while other actions will be taken behind the scenes at the law office or the courthouse.

Your attorney may perform any of the following tasks on your behalf:

- Assess the case to determine which court(s) have jurisdiction to hear the matter
- Develop a strategy for advising you about all aspects of your divorce, including the treatment of assets and matters regarding children
- Prepare legal documents for filing with the court

- Conduct discovery to obtain information from the other party, which could include depositions, requests for production of documents, and written interrogatories
- Appear with you at all court appearances, depositions, and conferences
- Schedule all deadlines and court appearances
- Support you in responding to information requests from your spouse
- Inform you of actions you are required to take
- Perform financial analyses of your case, sometimes with the help of outside "experts" such as appraisers, forensic accountants, tax professionals, and the like
- Conduct legal research
- Prepare you for court appearances and depositions
- Prepare your case for hearings and trial, including preparing exhibits and interviewing witnesses
- Advise you regarding your rights under the law
- Counsel you regarding the costs and benefits along with possible risks and rewards of a negotiated settlement as compared to proceeding to trial

As your advocate, your attorney is entrusted to take all of the steps necessary to represent your interests in the divorce.

3.5 What professionals might the court appoint to work with my attorney?

In some cases where custody or parenting time issues are seriously disputed, the court may appoint an attorney for the child or children, or a *guardian ad litem (GAL)*. A guardian *ad litem* "stands in the shoes" of the child and investigates you and your spouse as well as the needs of your child. She or he may then be called as a witness at trial to testify regarding any relevant observations and is subject to being cross-examined as is any other witness.

The *attorney for child* is just what you might think from the title. He or she is the child's attorney and is obligated to advocate for the child's position, as voiced by the child. The attorney is not permitted to substitute his or her judgment for that of the child. If you have two children it is possible for each child to have her or his own attorney as their interests/positions may differ.

In some cases a court may appoint a mental health forensic expert who is usually a psychologist or psychiatrist. The role of the mental health forensic expert will depend upon the purpose for which she or he was appointed. For example, the expert may be appointed to perform a child-custody evaluation, which involves assessing both parents and the child, or this expert may be ordered to evaluate one parent to access a child's safety while spending time with that parent.

The costs of these people (guardians *ad litem,* attorneys for children, and mental health forensics) are ordinarily paid by you and your spouse in proportions directed by the court.

3.6   I've been divorced before and I don't think I need an attorney this time; however, my spouse is hiring one. Is it wise to go it alone?

Having gone through a prior divorce, it's likely that you have learned a great deal about the divorce process as well as your legal rights, at least as they existed at that time. However, there are many reasons why you should be extremely cautious about proceeding without legal representation.

It is important to remember that every divorce is different. The length of the marriage, whether there are children, the relative financial situation for you and your spouse, as well as your age and health can all affect the financial outcome in your divorce.

The law may have changed since your last divorce. Some aspects of divorce law are likely to change each year. New laws get passed and new decisions get handed down by the courts that affect the rights and responsibilities of people who divorce. Tax laws change frequently and there may be some very specific methods of handling certain assets, which, if not followed, could lead to the imposition of significant costs.

In some cases, the involvement of your lawyer could be minimal. This might be the case if your marriage was short, your financial situation very similar to that of your spouse, there are no children, and the two of you remain amicable. At a minimum, have an initial consultation with an attorney to discuss your rights and have an attorney review any final agreement.

3.7   Can I take my children to meetings with my attorney?

For a number of reasons, it's best to make other arrangements for your children when you meet with your attorney. First of all, your attorney will be giving you a great deal of important information during your conferences, and it will benefit you to give your full attention.

Secondly, you should take every measure to keep information about the legal aspects of your divorce away from your children. This is a grown-up problem to be handled by grown-ups. Knowledge that you are seeing an attorney can add to your child's anxiety about the process. It can also make your child a target for questioning by the other parent about your contacts with your attorney.

Finally, on a practical level, most law offices are not designed to accommodate young children and are ordinarily not "child-proofed." For both your child's well-being and your own peace of mind, explore options for someone to care for your child when you have meetings with your attorney.

3.8   What is the role of the paralegal, or legal assistant, in my attorney's office?

A paralegal, or legal assistant, is a trained legal professional whose duties include providing support for you and your lawyer. Working with a paralegal can make your divorce easier because he or she is likely to be very available to help you. It can also lower your legal costs, considering the hourly rate for paralegal services is less than the rate for attorneys.

A paralegal is prohibited from giving legal advice. It is important that you respect the limits of the role of the paralegal if he or she is unable to answer your question because it calls for giving a legal opinion. However, a paralegal can answer many questions and provide a great deal of information to you throughout your divorce.

Paralegals can help you by receiving information from you, reviewing documents with you, providing you with updates on your case, and answering questions about the divorce process that do not call for legal advice.

3.9   My attorney is not returning my phone calls or e-mails. What can I do?

You have a right to expect that your lawyer respond to your phone calls and e-mails. Here are some options to consider:

- Ask to speak to the paralegal or another attorney in the office.

- Send an e-mail or fax telling your lawyer that you have been trying to reach him or her by phone and explaining the reason it is important that you receive a call.

- Ask the receptionist to schedule a phone conference for you to speak with your attorney at a specific date and time.

- Schedule a meeting with your attorney to discuss both the issue needing attention as well as your concerns about the communication problem.

Your attorney wants to provide good service to you. If your calls are not being returned, take action to get the communication with your lawyer back on track.

3.10   How do I know when it's time to change lawyers?

Although technically it's an easy thing to do, changing lawyers is costly and should not be done lightly. You will incur legal fees for your new attorney to review information that is already familiar to your current attorney. You will spend time giving much of the same information to your new lawyer as the one you have discharged. There will also be information that your previous attorney has which just can't be effectively given to the new attorney, such as her or his impression of a judge's attitude toward a legal theory or the thinking behind choosing one expert over another. A change in lawyers often results in delays in the divorce.

The following are questions to ask yourself when you're deciding whether to stay with your attorney or seek new counsel:

- Have I spoken directly to my attorney about my concerns?

- When I expressed concerns, did my lawyer take action accordingly?
- Is my lawyer open and receptive to what I have to say?
- Am I blaming my lawyer for the bad behavior of my spouse or opposing counsel?
- Have I provided my lawyer the information needed for taking the next action?
- Does my lawyer have control over the complaints I have, or are they ruled by the law or the judge?
- Is my lawyer keeping promises for completing action on my case?
- Do I trust my lawyer?
- What would be the advantages of changing lawyers when compared to the costs?
- Do I believe my lawyer will support me to achieve the outcome I'm seeking in my divorce?

Every effort should be made to resolve dissatisfaction with your attorney. If you have made this effort and the situation remains unchanged, it may be time to switch lawyers.

4

Attorney Fees and Costs

Anytime you make a major investment, you want to know what the cost is going to be and what you are getting for your money. Investing in quality legal representation for your divorce is no different.

The cost of your divorce might be one of your greatest concerns. Because of this, you will want to be an intelligent consumer of legal services. You want quality, but you also want to get the best value for the fees you are paying.

Legal fees for a divorce can be costly and the total expense not always predictable. But there are many actions you can take to control and estimate the cost. Develop a plan early on for how you will finance your divorce. Speak openly with your lawyer about fees from the outset. Learn as much as you can about how you will be charged. New York law requires that the fee agreement be in writing and that you be provided with a statement of client rights and responsibilities.

By being informed, aware, and wise, your financial investment in your divorce will be money well spent to protect your future.

4.1 Can I get free legal advice from a lawyer over the phone?

Every law firm has its own policy regarding lawyers talking to people who are not yet clients of the firm. Most questions about your divorce are too complex for a lawyer to give a meaningful answer during a brief phone call.

39

Answers to your questions about your divorce require a complete look at the facts, circumstances, and background of your marriage. To obtain good legal advice, it's best to schedule an initial consultation with a lawyer who handles divorces.

4.2 Will I be charged for the initial consultation with a lawyer?

It depends. Some lawyers give free consultations, whereas others charge a fee. When scheduling your appointment, you should be told the amount of the fee. Payment is ordinarily due at the time of the consultation.

4.3 Will I be expected to give money to the attorney after our first meeting? If so, how much?

If your attorney charges for an initial consultation, be prepared to make payment at the time of your meeting. At the close of your consultation, the attorney may tell you the amount of the retainer needed by the law firm to handle your divorce. However, you are not expected to pay the retainer at the time of your first meeting. Rather, the retainer is paid after you have accepted the lawyer and the lawyer has accepted your case and you have signed a written retainer agreement.

4.4 What exactly is a retainer and how much will mine be?

A retainer is a sum paid to your lawyer in advance for services to be performed and costs to be incurred in your divorce. It is a deposit. This will either be an amount paid toward a *flat-fee* cost for your divorce or an advance credit for services that will be charged by the hour.

If you decide to hire the lawyer and your case is accepted by the law firm, expect the attorney to request a retainer following the initial consultation. The amount of the retainer depends upon the nature of your case. Contested custody, divorces involving businesses, or interstate disputes, for example, are all likely to require higher retainers.

Other factors that can affect the amount of the retainer include the nature and number of the disputed issues, the degree of conflict between the parties, and the anticipated overall cost of the litigation.

New York does not permit the retainer to be nonrefundable. The use of the retainer, the possible minimum fee, and all other financial rights and obligations are set forth in the written retainer agreement, in addition to your rights in the event of a dispute with your lawyer about the fees charged.

4.5 I don't have any money and I need a divorce. What are my options?

Two factors to consider in your situation are time and money.

Let's look at money first. If your income is very low and your assets are few, you may be eligible to obtain a divorce at no cost or minimal cost through a program supported by a local bar association or a law school at a nearby university.

These organizations have a screening process for potential clients, as well as limits on the nature of the cases they take. The demand for their services is also usually greater than the number of attorneys available to handle cases. Consequently, if you are eligible for legal services from one of these programs, you should anticipate being on a waiting list. In short, if you have very little income and few assets, you are likely to experience some delay in obtaining a lawyer. If you believe you might be eligible for participation in one of these programs, inquire early to increase your opportunity to get the legal help you are seeking in a timely manner.

4.6 I don't have much money, but I need to get a divorce as quickly as possible. What should I do?

If you have some money and want to a divorce as soon as possible, consider some of these options:

- Borrow the legal fees.
- Charge the legal fees on a low-interest credit card.
- Talk with your attorney about using money held in a joint account with your spouse.
- Find an attorney who will work with you on a monthly payment basis.
- Ask your attorney about your spouse paying for your legal fees.

Even if you do not have the financial resources to proceed with your divorce at this time, consult with an attorney to learn your rights and to develop an action plan for steps you can take between now and the time you are able to proceed.

Often there are measures you can take right away to protect yourself until you have the money to proceed with your divorce.

4.7 Is there anything I can do on my own to get support for my children if I don't have money for a lawyer for a divorce?

Yes. If you need support for your children, you can make an application in the Family Court. This court does not have the jurisdiction to grant a divorce or affect title to property but it can handle other aspects of child and spousal support and child custody along with orders of protection. Family Courts in New York are very familiar with unrepresented parties.

4.8 How much does it cost to get a divorce?

Like so many other answers, the answer to this question is: "It depends." Some attorneys perform divorces for a flat fee, but most charge by the hour. A flat fee is a fixed amount for the legal services being provided. A flat fee is more likely to be used when there are no children of the marriage and the parties have agreed upon the division of their property and debts. Most New York attorneys charge by the hour for work on divorce cases.

It is important that your discussion of the cost of your divorce begin at your first meeting with your attorney.

4.9 What are typical hourly rates for a divorce lawyer?

Hourly rates for New York attorneys vary greatly with their reputation, skills, and the amount of experience and the location. Lawyers in the larger cities charge more because their overhead is more. Young lawyers charge less than more-experienced attorneys.

If you have a concern about an attorney's hourly rate, but you would like to hire the firm with which the attorney is associated, consider asking to work with an associate attorney in the firm who is likely to charge a lower rate. Associates are attorneys who ordinarily have less experience than the senior partners. However, they often are trained by the senior partners, experienced, and capable of handling your case.

4.10 Can I make payments to my attorney?

Every law firm has its own policies regarding payment arrangements for divorce clients. Often these arrangements are tailored to the specific client. Most attorneys will require a substantial retainer to be paid at the outset of your case. Some attorneys may accept monthly payments in lieu of the retainer. Others may require monthly payments or request additional retainers as your case progresses. Ask frank questions of your attorney to have clarity about your responsibility for payment of legal fees.

4.11 I've been turned down by programs providing free legal services. How can I get the money to pay for a lawyer?

There are a number of options to consider when it looks as though you are without funds to pay an attorney.

First, ask yourself whether you have closely examined all sources of funds readily available to you. Sometimes you may have simply overlooked money that you might be able to access with ease.

Next, talk to your family members and friends. Often those close to you are concerned about your future and would be very pleased to support you in your goal of having your rights protected. Although this may be uncomfortable to do, remember that most people will appreciate that you trusted them enough to ask for their help. If the retainer is too much money to request from a single individual, consider whether a handful of persons might each be able to contribute a lesser amount to help you reach your goal of hiring a lawyer.

If your case is not urgent, consider developing a plan for saving the money you need to proceed with a divorce. Your attorney may be willing to receive and hold monthly payments until you have paid in an amount sufficient to pay the initial retainer.

Consider taking out a loan or charging your retainer on a credit card.

Under certain circumstances, an attorney might be willing to be paid from the proceeds of a property settlement. If you and your spouse have acquired substantial assets during the marriage, you may be able to find an attorney who will wait to be paid until the assets are divided at the conclusion of the divorce.

Finally, in New York and a few other jurisdictions, there are businesses that are specifically set up to lend money to individuals for legal expenses and living expenses while going through a divorce. These businesses can be very helpful in providing liquidity when your family's assets are tied up in a home, a retirement, and/or the value of a business.

4.12 I agreed to pay my attorney a substantial retainer to begin my case. Will I still have to make monthly payments?

Your financial obligations to your attorney are fully described in the required retainer agreement. You should read it carefully and understand it fully before you sign it.

4.13 My lawyer gave me an estimate of the cost of my divorce and it sounds reasonable. Do I still need a written fee agreement?

The requirement of having a written fee agreement is imposed by law. You cannot hire an attorney without a written agreement.

4.14 How will I know how the fees and charges are accumulating?

Your attorney is required by law to send you an itemized bill at least every sixty days. If he or she does not do so, your attorney could be prevented from seeking payment. If your attorney agrees to handle your divorce for a flat fee, your fee agreement should clearly set forth what is included in the fee.

Review your bill promptly after you receive it. Check to make sure there are no errors, such as duplicate billing entries. If your statement reflects work that you were unaware was performed, call for clarification. Your attorney's office should welcome any questions you have about services it provided.

Your statement might also include filing fees, court reporter fees for transcripts of court testimony or depositions, copy expenses, or interest charged on your account.

There are certain time limits for you to register your disagreement regarding any bills you receive. If you don't make your objections known within the time limit, you might lose your right to object later. Your attorney is not permitted to charge you for time taken to explain her bills.

4.15 What other expenses are related to the divorce litigation besides lawyer fees?

Talk to your attorney about costs other than the attorney fees. Ask whether it is likely there will be filing fees, court reporter expenses, subpoenas, or expert-witness fees. Expert-witness fees can be a substantial expense ranging from hundreds to thousands of dollars, depending upon the type of expert and the extent to which he or she is involved in your case.

Speak frankly with your attorney about these costs so that together you can make the best decisions about how to use your budget for the litigation.

4.16 Who pays for the experts such as the appraiser, the accountant, and the psychologist?

Costs for the services of experts, whether appointed by the court or hired by the parties, are ordinarily paid for by the parties.

In the case of the guardian *ad litem* or an attorney for a child, the amount of the fee will depend upon how much time this professional spends. The judge often orders this fee to be shared in some fashion by the parties. Sometimes it is shared equally, sometimes proportionally based on income. However, depending upon the circumstances one party can be ordered to pay the entire fee.

Mental health forensic experts either charge by the hour or can set a flat fee for a certain type of evaluation. Again, the court can order one party to pay this fee or both parties to share the expense. The court usually requires that a retainer payment be made in advance and the expert will often refuse to issue a report until all fees are paid.

The fees for many experts, including appraisers and accountants, will vary depending upon whether the individuals are called upon to provide only a specific service such as an appraisal, or whether they will need to prepare for giving testimony and appear as a witness at trial.

Don't forget that regardless of who pays these fees, the money spent is money that might otherwise be available for your family.

4.17 What factors will impact how much my divorce will cost?

Although it is difficult to predict how much your legal fees will be, the following are some of the factors that affect the cost:

- Whether there are children
- Whether child custody is agreed upon
- Whether there are novel legal questions
- Whether there are businesses or professional attainments that need to be valued
- Whether a pension plan will be divided between the parties
- The nature of the issues contested
- The cooperation of the opposing party and opposing counsel
- Whether there are litigation costs, such as fees for expert witnesses or court reporters
- The hourly rate of the attorney

Communicating with your lawyer regularly about your legal fees will help you to have a better understanding of the overall cost as your case proceeds.

4.18 Will my attorney charge for phone calls and e-mails?

Unless your case is being handled on a flat-fee basis, you should expect to be billed for phone calls with your attorney. Many of the professional services provided by lawyers are done by phone and by e-mail. This time can be spent giving legal advice, negotiating, or gathering information to protect your interests. These calls and e-mails are all legal services for which you should anticipate being charged by your attorney.

To make the most of your time during attorney phone calls, plan your call in advance. Organize the information you want to relay, your questions, and any concerns to be addressed. This will help you to be clear and focused during the phone call so that your fees are well spent.

4.19   Will I be charged for talking to the staff at my lawyer's office?

It depends. Check the terms of your fee agreement with your lawyer. Whether you are charged fees for talking to nonlawyer members of the law office may depend upon their role in the office. For example, many law firms charge for the services of paralegals and law clerks.

Remember that nonlawyers cannot give legal advice and you should respect these limitations. Don't expect the receptionist to give you an opinion regarding whether you will win custody or receive maintenance.

Your lawyer's support staff will be able to relay your messages and receive information from you. They may also be able to answer many of your questions. Allowing support from nonattorneys in the firm is one way to control your legal fees, too.

4.20   What is a trial retainer and will I have to pay one?

A *trial retainer* is a sum of money paid toward your account with your lawyer when it becomes apparent that your case will not settle and is proceeding to trial.

The purpose of the trial retainer is to fund the work needed to prepare for trial and for services the day or days of trial.

Confirm with your attorney that any unearned portion of your trial retainer will be refunded if your case settles. Whether and when a trial retainer might be required in your case is set forth in your retainer agreement.

4.21 How do I know whether I should spend the attorney fees my lawyer says is required to take my case to trial?

Deciding whether to take a case to trial or to settle is often the most challenging point in the divorce process. This decision should be made with the advice of your attorney.

When the issues in dispute are primarily financial, often the decision about settlement is related to the costs of going to trial. Clarify just how far apart you and your spouse are on the financial matters and compare this to the estimated costs of going to trial. By comparing these amounts, you can decide whether to compromise on certain financial issues. This will be better than paying legal fees and not knowing how your case will resolve.

4.22 If my mother pays my legal fees, will my lawyer give her private information about my divorce?

Not without your clear permission.

Even if someone other than you is paying your legal bills, your lawyer must honor the ethical duty to maintain confidentiality. Without your permission, your attorney should not be disclosing information to others about your case unless you consent to it.

If you do want your lawyer to be able to communicate with your family members, advise your lawyer and ask your lawyer if communications with these people might affect the attorney-client privilege. Expect to be charged by your lawyer for the time spent on these calls or meetings. Regardless of the opinions of the person who pays your attorney fees, your lawyer's duty is to remain your zealous advocate.

4.23 Can I ask the court to order my spouse to pay my attorney fees?

Yes. New York law states that there is a legal presumption that the "less monied spouse" shall be awarded fees in a timely fashion in order to ensure "adequate representation." Be sure to discuss this obligation with your attorney at the first opportunity. Most lawyers will treat the obligation for your legal fees as yours unless the other party has been ordered or agreed to make the payment.

If your case is likely to require costly experts and your spouse has a much greater ability to pay these expenses than you do, talk to your lawyer about the possibility of filing a motion with the court asking your spouse to pay toward these costs while the case is pending.

4.24 What happens if I don't pay my attorney the fees I promised to pay?

The ethical rules for lawyers allow your attorney to withdraw from representation if you do not comply with your fee agreement. If your case is pending in a court, your attorney may have to ask the court for permission to withdraw. Consequently, it is important that you keep the promises you have made regarding your account.

If you are having difficulty paying your attorneys fees, talk with your attorney about payment options. Consider borrowing the funds, using your credit card, or asking for help from friends and family.

Above all, do not avoid communication with your attorney if you are having difficulties making payment. Keeping in touch with your attorney is essential for you to have an advocate at all stages of your divorce.

4.25 Is there any way I can reduce some of the expenses of getting a divorce?

Litigation of any kind can be expensive, and divorces are no exception. The good news is that there are many ways that you can help to control the expense. Here are some of them.

Put it in writing. If you need to relay information that is important but not urgent, consider providing it to your attorney by mail, fax, or e-mail. This creates a prompt and accurate record for your file and your lawyer's in less time than exchanging phone messages and talking on the phone.

Keep your attorney informed. Just as your attorney should keep you up to date on the status of your case, you need to do the same. Keep your lawyer advised about any major developments in your life such as plans to move, to have someone move into your home, to change your employment status, to start a business, or to buy or sell property. Any significant change in your financial circumstances or personal life should be reported to your attorney. Any major development regarding your children should be reported as well.

During a divorce, your address, phone numbers, or e-mail address may change. Be sure to let your attorney know. Often, timely advice on the part of your lawyer can avoid more costly fees later.

Obtain copies of documents. An important part of litigation includes reviewing documents such as tax returns, account statements, report cards, or medical records. Your attorney will ordinarily be able to request or subpoena these items, but many may be readily available to you directly upon request.

Consult your attorney's website. If your lawyer has a website, it may be a great source of useful information. The answers to commonly asked questions about the divorce process can often be found there.

Utilize support professionals. Get to know the support staff at your lawyer's office. The receptionist, paralegal, legal secretary, or law clerk may have the answer to your question. Only the attorneys in the office are able to give you legal advice, but other professionals in the law office can often provide answers to questions regarding the status of your case. Just as your communication with your attorney, all communication with any professionals in a law firm is required to be kept strictly confidential.

Consider working with an associate attorney. Although the senior attorneys or partners in a law firm may have more experience, you may find that working with an associate attorney is a good option. Hourly rates for an associate attorney are typically lower than those charged by a senior partner. Frequently, the associate attorney has trained under a senior partner and developed excellent skills as well as the knowledge of the law. Many associate attorneys are also very experienced.

Discuss with the firm the benefits of working with a senior attorney or an associate attorney in light of the nature of your case, the expertise of the respective attorneys, and the potential cost savings to you.

Leave a detailed message. If your attorney knows the information you are seeking, she or he can often get the answer before returning your call. This not only gets your answer faster, but also reduces costs.

Discuss more than one matter during a call. It is not unusual for clients to have many questions during litigation. If your question is not urgent, consider waiting to call until you have more than one inquiry. Never hesitate to call to ask any legal questions.

Provide timely responses to information requests. Whenever possible, provide information requested by your lawyer in a timely manner. This avoids the cost of follow-up action by your lawyer and the additional expense of extending the time in litigation.

Carefully review your monthly statements. Scrutinize your monthly billing statements closely. If you believe an error has been made, contact your lawyer's office right away to discuss your concerns. You will not be charged for time spent discussing your bill.

Remain open to settlement. A disagreement over smaller sums of money may cost more in legal fees to take to court than the value of what is disputed. By remaining open to settlement, you can use your legal fees wisely and control the costs of your divorce.

5

The Discovery Process

Discovery is one of the least talked about steps in divorce, but it is often among the most important. The purpose of discovery is to ensure that both you and your spouse have access to the same information. In this way, you can either negotiate a fair agreement or have all of the facts and documents to present to the judge at trial.

You and your spouse both need the same information if you hope to reach agreement on any of the issues in your divorce. Similarly, the judge must know all of the facts to make a fair decision. The discovery process may seem tedious at times because of the need to obtain and to provide a lot of detailed information. Completing it, however, can give tremendous clarity about the issues in your divorce. Trust your lawyer's advice about the importance of having the necessary evidence as you complete the discovery process in order to reach your goals in your divorce.

5.1   What is *discovery*?

Discovery is that part of your divorce process in which the attorneys attempt to learn as much about the facts of your case as possible. Through a variety of methods, both lawyers will request information from you, your spouse, and potential witnesses in your case.

5.2 What types of discovery might be done by my lawyer or my spouse's lawyer?

Types of discovery include:

- *Interrogatories*—which are written questions that must be answered under oath
- *Requests for production of documents*—asking that certain documents be provided by you or your spouse
- *Requests for admissions*—asking that certain facts be admitted or denied
- *Subpoena of documents*
- *Depositions*—in which questions are asked and answered in the presence of a court reporter but outside of the presence of a judge
- *Physical examinations*—if someone has health issues or claims some sort of disability
- *Vocational examinations*—to determine someone's earning capacity

Factors that can influence the type of discovery conducted include:

- The issues in dispute
- How much access you and your spouse have to needed information
- The level of cooperation in sharing information
- The budget available for performing discovery

Talk to your lawyer about the nature and extent of discovery anticipated in your case.

5.3 How long does the discovery process take?

Discovery can take anywhere from a few weeks to many months, depending upon factors such as the complexity of the case, the cooperation of you and your spouse, and whether expert witnesses are involved.

New York law provides for a number of deadlines for different types of discovery divorces. Your lawyer will be able to tell you about them.

5.4 My lawyer insists that we conduct discovery, but I don't want to spend the time and money on it. Is it really necessary?

In a word: "Yes."

The discovery process can be critical to a successful outcome in your case for several reasons:

- It increases the likelihood that any agreements reached are based upon accurate information.

- It provides necessary information for deciding whether to settle or proceed to trial.

- It supports the preparation of defenses by providing information regarding your spouse's case.

- It avoids surprises at trial, such as unexpected witness testimony.

Discuss with your attorney the intention behind the discovery being conducted in your case to ensure it is consistent with your goals and a meaningful investment of your legal fees.

5.5 I just received from my spouse's attorney interrogatories and requests that I produce documents. My lawyer wants me to respond within two weeks. I'll never make the deadline. What can I do?

First, take a deep breath. Receiving a mountain of unfamiliar documents can be very disorienting. Remember, though, that answering your discovery promptly will help move your case forward and help control your legal fees. There are steps you can take to make this task less daunting and easier.

Look at all of the questions. Many of them may not apply or your answers will be a simple "yes" or "no." It is not uncommon for a lawyer to use a "standard" set of demands, trying to make one size fit every case.

Ask a friend to help you. It is important that you develop the practice of letting others help you while you are going through your divorce. Chances are that you will make great progress in just a couple of hours with a friend helping you.

Break it down into smaller tasks. If you answer just a few questions a day, the job will not be so overwhelming.

Call your lawyer. Ask whether a paralegal in the office can help you organize the needed information or determine whether some of it can be provided at a later date.

Delay in the discovery process often leads to frustration by clients and lawyers. Do your best to provide the information in a timely manner with the help of others.

5.6   My spouse's lawyer intends to subpoena my medical records. Aren't these private?

Whether or not your medical records are relevant in your case will depend upon the issues in dispute. If you are requesting support or if your health is an issue in the dispute of child custody, these records may be relevant.

Talk with your lawyer about your rights. It may be that a motion to limit or dismiss the demands is needed.

5.7   It's been two months since my lawyer sent interrogatories to my spouse, and we still don't have his answers. I answered mine on time. Is there anything that can be done to speed up the process?

The failure or refusal of a spouse to follow the rules of discovery can add to both the frustration and expense of the divorce process.

Talk with your attorney about filing a motion to compel, seeking a court order requiring your spouse to provide the requested information by a certain date. A request for attorney fees for the filing of the motion may also be appropriate.

Ask your lawyer whether a subpoena of information from an employer or a financial institution would be a more cost-effective way to get needed facts and documents if your spouse remains uncooperative.

Ultimately, if your spouse refuses to provide information that is available, she or he may be precluded from introducing evidence or contesting certain facts at trial.

5.8   What is a deposition?

A *deposition* is the asking and answering of questions under oath, outside of court, in the presence of a court reporter. A deposition may be taken of you, your spouse, or certain potential witnesses in your divorce case. Both attorneys will be present. You and your spouse also have the right to be present during the taking of depositions of each other and any witnesses in your case. Depositions are performed in most divorces.

After your deposition is completed, the questions and answers will be transcribed, that is, typed, by the court reporter exactly as given and bound into one or more volumes.

Any witness who testifies at the deposition will be given a chance to review the transcript and correct it to the extent that you point out that something that was said was improperly transcribed. The witness does not get to change the answers.

5.9   What is the purpose of a deposition?

A deposition can serve a number of purposes, such as:

- Supporting the settlement process by providing valuable information

- Helping your attorney determine who to use as witnesses at trial

- Aiding in the assessment of a witness's credibility, that is, whether the witness appears to be telling the truth

- Helping avoid surprise at trial by learning the testimony of witnesses in advance

- Preserving testimony in the event the witness becomes unavailable for trial

Depositions can be essential tools in a divorce, especially when a case is likely to proceed to trial.

5.10   Will what I say in my deposition be used against me when we go to court?

Usually, a deposition is used to develop trial strategy and obtain information in preparation for trial. In some circumstances, a deposition may be used at trial.

If you are later called to testify as a witness and give testimony contrary to your deposition, your deposition can be used to impeach you by showing the inconsistency in your statements. It is important to review your deposition prior to your live testimony to ensure consistency and prepare yourself for the type of questions you may be asked.

5.11 Will the judge read the depositions?

Unless a witness becomes unavailable for trial or gives conflicting testimony at trial, it is unlikely that the judge will ever read the depositions. However, excerpts from a deposition transcript are sometimes included in motion papers.

5.12 How should I prepare for my deposition?

To prepare for your deposition, review important documents. These include the complaint, your answers to interrogatories, your net worth statement, any affidavits or documents submitted for connection with any materials, and your financial documents that have been provided to the other side.

Talk to your attorney about the type of questions you can expect to be asked. Discuss any questions you are concerned about answering.

5.13 What will I be asked? Can I refuse to answer questions?

Questions in a deposition can cover a broad range of topics including your education, work, income, expenses, assets, liabilities, and family. The attorney is allowed to ask reasonable questions that may lead to the discovery of admissible evidence. If the question may lead to relevant information, it can be asked in a deposition, even though it may be inadmissible at trial. Your attorney may object to the "form" of the question (usually a question that assumes a fact such as "When did you stop drinking excessively?"). Your attorney may only direct you not to answer a question that would require you to give information that may be *privileged*.

Depending on where your case is pending, there may be other restrictions on the areas of inquiry so you should be sure to ask your attorney about these restrictions.

5.14 What if I give incorrect information in my deposition?

You will be under oath so it is important that you be truthful. If you give incorrect information by mistake, contact your attorney as soon as you realize the error. If you lie during your deposition, you risk being impeached by the other lawyer during your divorce trial. At a minimum, this could cause you to lose credibility with the court, rendering your testimony less valuable.

5.15 What if I don't know or can't remember the answer to a question?

You may be asked questions about which you have no knowledge. It is always acceptable to say "I don't know" if you do not have the knowledge. Similarly, if you cannot remember, simply say so.

Your attorney will likely tell you not to guess or estimate. Your deposition is not the place for you to try and win your case.

5.16 What else do I need to know about having my deposition taken?

The following suggestions will help you give a successful deposition:

- Prepare for your deposition by reviewing and providing necessary documents and talking with your lawyer.

- Get a good night's sleep. Eat a meal with protein to sustain your energy.

- Arrive early so that you have time to get comfortable with your surroundings.

- Relax. You are going to be asked questions about matters you know about. Your deposition is likely to begin with routine matters such as your education and work history.

- Tell the truth, including whether you have met with an attorney or discussed preparation for the deposition.

- Stay calm. Your spouse's lawyer will be judging your credibility and demeanor. Do not argue with the attorneys.

- Listen carefully to the entire question. Do not try to anticipate questions or start thinking about your answer before the attorney has finished asking the question.

- Answer the question directly. If the question calls only for "yes" or "no," provide such an answer.

- Do not volunteer information. If the lawyer wants to elicit more information, he or she will do so in following questions.

- If you do not understand the question clearly, ask that it be repeated or rephrased. Do not try to answer what you *think* was asked.
- Take your time and carefully consider the question before answering. There is no need to hurry.
- If you do not know or cannot remember the answer, say so. That is an adequate answer.
- Do not guess.
- Do not let an attorney pin you down to anything you are not sure about. For example, if you cannot remember the number of times an event occurred, say that. If the attorney asks you to estimate, don't. However, if you can provide a range (such as: more than ten but less than twenty) with reasonable certainty, you may do so.
- If an attorney mischaracterizes something you said earlier, say so.
- Speak clearly and loudly enough for everyone to hear you.
- Answer all questions with words, rather than gestures or sounds. "Uh-huh" is difficult for the court report to distinguish from "unh-unh" and may result in inaccuracies in the transcript.
- If you need a break at any point in the deposition, you have a right to request one. You can talk to your attorney during such a break, so long as there is not an open question.

5.17 Are depositions always necessary? Does every witness have to be deposed?

Depositions are less likely to be needed if you and your spouse are reaching agreement on most of the facts in your case and you are moving toward a settlement. They are more likely to be needed in cases where there are complex financial issues or many areas of disagreement.

5.18 Will I get a copy of the depositions in my case?

Yes.

6

Mediation and Negotiation

If you have decided that your marriage is going to end, the first *process* you will experience will be some sort of negotiation. I say "process" because I don't believe that every couples' negotiations will follow the same path, in the same order, at the same time intervals.

You and your spouse have developed your own marriage narrative and conversation over time, and you and your spouse will, most likely, resolve your divorce issues via your own negotiation conversation. When I wrote "most likely," I meant that because 90 percent or more of the marriages ending in New York are resolved by an agreement between the parties, it si most likely that you will reach an agreement as well.

That is not to say that your negotiation process won't involve some sort of court involvement. Sometimes it is helpful to negotiate in the shadow of a court proceeding because the structured nature of a litigation can provide boundaries for the negotiations. Limits will not only be placed on the positions taken, but there will be firm deadlines by which agreements must be made, or tasks accomplished, *or else*.

In order to begin a negotiation you need to know what it is you are negotiating about. Some issues are obvious because they are in front of you all day, every day, like matters addressing your children. But it is helpful to start with an organized assembly of your income, your assets, your expenses, and your debts along with any other additional information you may be asked to gather by your attorney.

You need to work with your attorney to set realistic and specific goals. You need to be aware of what are the strengths and what are the weaknesses of your case. For example, if you work 60 to 70 hours a week, or if your job requires that you travel out of town with some frequency, you need to ask yourself if having your children with you for 50 percent of the time is realistic. If your spouse earns $120,000 per year before taxes and you earn $60,000, is it reasonable to think that you will now be able to maintain two separate households and keep the children in private schools and sleep-away camps? If you have been the sole caregiver of the children, made every appointment, took them to every play date, went by yourself to every parent-teacher conference, and you were the only one to take days off to stay home when they were sick, should you really be worried that your spouse will get sole custody of the children?

Your attorney will help you separate the "real" from the "ideal" so that even if you don't end up with what you "want," you can achieve a result that you understand to be within a zone of fairness and reality.

Once you have gathered the information you have and come to some understanding of your goals, you can open up specific discussions with your spouse, either directly or through your respective attorneys. There may be some information that should be exchanged so that everyone is working from the same page(s), and then its time for you each to listen.

You need to listen in order to hear what your spouse feels is really important to her or him, and then think if there is a way to give her or him something he or she wants that might not be so important to you, in order to get something you want in exchange. You also need to evaluate the "shelf life" of what is being asked for. Your spouse may need you to cooperate in taking advantage of a relatively short-lived opportunity. If you delay for too long, or try to get more than it's worth in exchange, the opportunity for your spouse may lapse, and the chance you had to make a good trade has lapsed with it.

Once you've heard what your spouse wants, you should consider making a proposal or asking for a proposal. As long as you each feel you are making progress, the discussions continue and the revisions to the proposals and counter-proposals continue. There is no rule as to how long you and your spouse can participate in this process. The negotiations will end when one of two things happens:

- You have made a deal
- Someone decides that the negotiation process has run its course.

If you have made a deal, an attorney drafts the settlement agreement, provides it to the other attorney for review and comment. This document gets revised as needed until everyone agrees that it embodies the terms of the agreement reached. The agreement is signed and, if you want to get divorced, appropriate court filings are prepared and submitted. Sometimes you may not want to get divorced right away. It is possible that someone's health insurance plan will continue to cover the other spouse so long as he or she is still a spouse. In that case it may not be worth it to get divorced right away. This is a decision you all need to make together because remaining married has a number of consequences. For example, you cannot marry anyone else and you must file a tax return as a married person (whether jointly or separately).

If the negotiations end without an agreement, your next likely step is to start a divorce lawsuit. However, you never lose the opportunity to negotiate and the odds are that even if you get involved in a litigation, your negotiations will resume and it is most likely that your divorce will still be resolved by an agreement.

6.1 What is the difference between mediation and negotiation?

Both *mediation* and *negotiation* are methods used to help you and your spouse settle your divorce by reaching an agreement rather than going to trial and having the judge make decisions for you. These methods are sometimes referred to as types of *alternative dispute resolution* or *ADR*.

Mediation uses a trained mediator who is an independent, neutral third party. He or she is a skilled professional who can assist you and your spouse in the process. Negotiation ordinarily involves lawyers for both you and your spouse. Lawyers for the spouses may also be present or in the background during mediation, although their involvement is usually less than in negotiation.

6.2   How are mediation and negotiation different from a collaborative divorce?

Collaborative law is a technique for trying to resolve a divorce case where both parties have a strong commitment to settling their disputes and avoiding litigation. You and your spouse each hire an attorney trained in the collaborative law process. A key feature of the protocol is that you, your spouse, and your representative lawyers enter into an agreement providing that, in the event either you or your spouse decides to take the case to court, both of you must terminate services with your collaborative lawyers and start anew.

Often, spouses in the collaborative process enlist the support of other professionals, such as an independent financial advisor or coaches, to support them through the process. Although the process may be lengthy, it enables the focus to shift away from the conflict and toward finding solutions.

Talk to your lawyer about whether your case would be well suited to the collaborative law process.

6.3   What is involved in the mediation process? What will I have to do and how long will it take?

The mediation process will be explained to you in detail by the mediator at the start of the mediation process. Mediation involves one or more meetings with you, your spouse, and the mediator. In some cases the attorneys will also be present.

The mediator will outline ground rules designed to ensure you will be treated respectfully and given an opportunity to be heard. In most cases you and your spouse will each be given an opportunity to make opening remarks about what is important to you in the outcome of the divorce.

How long the process of mediation continues depends upon many of the same factors that affect how long your divorce will take. These include how many issues you and your spouse disagree about, the complexity of these issues, the ease of exchanging relevant information, and the willingness of each of you to work toward an agreement.

Your case could settle after just a couple of mediation sessions or it might require a series of meetings. It is common for the mediator to clarify at the close of each session whether the parties are willing to continue with another session.

6.4 My lawyer said that mediation and negotiation can reduce delays in completing my divorce. How can they do this?

When the issues in your divorce are decided by a judge instead of by you and your spouse, there are many opportunities for delay. These can include:

- Waiting for a trial date
- Having to return to court on a later, second date if your trial is not completed on the day it is scheduled
- Waiting for the judge's ruling on your case
- Additional court hearings after your trial to resolve disputes about the intention of your judge's rulings, issues that were overlooked, or disagreement regarding language of the decree

Each one of these events holds the possibility of delaying your divorce by days, weeks, or even months. Mediating or negotiating the terms of your divorce decree can eliminate these delays.

6.5 How can mediation and negotiation lower the costs of my divorce?

If your case is not settled by agreement, you will be going to trial. If the issues in your case are many or if they are complex, such as business or career valuations or child custody, the attorney's fees and other costs of going to trial can be tremendous.

By settling your case without going to trial, you may be able to save thousands of dollars in legal fees. Ask your attorney for a litigation budget that sets forth the potential costs of going to trial, so that you have some idea of these costs when deciding whether to settle an issue or to take it to trial before the judge. A good rule of thumb is that each hour of trial will take two to three hours of preparation. So, a six-hour trial day will require twelve to eighteen hours of preparation.

At $500 per hour, a trial day would cost between $9,000 and $12,000.

6.6 Are there other benefits to mediating or negotiating a settlement?

Yes. A divorce resolved by a mediated or negotiated agreement can have these additional benefits:

Recognizing Common Goals. Mediation and negotiation allow for brainstorming between the parties and lawyers. Looking at all possible solutions, even the impractical ones, invites creative solutions to common goals. For example, suppose you and your spouse both agree that you need to pay your spouse some amount of equity for the family home you will keep, but you have no cash to make the payment. Together, you might come up with a number of options for accomplishing your goal and select the best one. Contrast this with the judge simply ordering you to pay the money without considering all of the possible options.

Addressing the Unique Circumstances of Your Situation. Rather than using the limited toolbox that is provided to the judge by law, a settlement reached by agreement allows you and your spouse to consider the unique circumstances of your situation in crafting a tailor-made outcome. For example, suppose you disagree about the parenting times for the Thanksgiving holiday. The judge might order you to alternate the holiday each year, even though you both would have preferred to have your child share the day.

Creating a Safe Place for Communication. Mediation and negotiation give each party an opportunity to be heard. Perhaps you and your spouse have not yet had an opportunity to share directly your concerns about settlement. For example, you might be worried about how the temporary parenting time arrangement is impacting your children, but have not yet talked to your spouse about it. A mediation session or settlement conference can be a safe place for you and your spouse to communicate your concerns about your children or your finances.

Fulfilling Your Children's Needs. You may see that your children would be better served by you and your spouse deciding their future rather than by a judge who does not know, love, and understand your children like the two of you do.

Eliminating the Risk and Uncertainty of Trial. If a judge decides the outcome of your divorce, you give up control over the terms of the settlement. The decisions are left in the hands of the judge. If you and your spouse reach agreement, however, you have the power to eliminate the risk of an uncertain outcome.

Reducing the Risk of Harm to Your Children. If your case goes to trial, it is likely that you and your spouse will give testimony that will be upsetting to each other. As the conflict increases, the relationship between you and your spouse inevitably deteriorates. This can be harmful to your children. Contrast this with mediation or settlement negotiations, in which you open your communication and seek to reach agreement. It is not unusual for the relationship between the parents to improve as the professionals create a safe environment for rebuilding communication and reaching agreements in the best interests of a child.

Having the Support of Professionals. Using trained professionals such as mediators and lawyers to support you can help you to reach a settlement that you might think is impossible. These professionals have skills to help you focus on what is most important to you and shift your attention away from irrelevant facts. They understand the law and know the possible outcomes if your case goes to trial.

Lowering Stress. The process of preparing for and going to court can be stressful. Your energy should be going toward caring for your children, looking at your finances, and coping with the emotions of divorce. You might decide that you would be better served by settling your case rather than proceeding to trial.

Achieving Closure. When you are going through a divorce, the process can feel as though it is taking an eternity. By reaching agreement, you and your spouse are better able to put the divorce behind you and move forward with your lives.

6.7   Is mediation mandatory?

As of this writing, there are a number of pilot programs to have people try mediation before they are too deeply engaged in litigation. But as of now, mediation is not required before the start of a divorce litigation.

6.8   What if I want to try mediation and my spouse doesn't?

You can't force your spouse into mediation.

6.9   My spouse abused me and I am afraid to participate in mediation. Should I participate anyway?

Mediation requires that the parties agree to speak openly and candidly in order to reach a fair agreement. If your spouse has abused you he or she is not likely to be committed to a process of self-guided fairness.

6.10   What training and credentials do mediators have?

The background of mediators varies. Some are attorneys; many come from other backgrounds such as counseling. Some mediators have received their training through recognized organizations like the American Academy of Matrimonial Lawyers, and others have not. A mediator is not required to have any particular training to call themselves divorce mediators. Ask your attorney for help in finding a qualified mediator.

6.11   What types of issues can be mediated or negotiated?

All of the issues in your case can be mediated or negotiated. However, in advance of any mediation or negotiation session, you should discuss with your lawyer which issues you want to be mediated or negotiated.

Talk with your lawyer in advance of any mediation that is limited to certain issues because an agreement on one issue may limit your options regarding others. For instance, agreeing to certain custody terms can reduce child support, and you should not negotiate on child custody and parenting time without having first fully discussed with your attorney its impact on child support.

You may decide that certain issues are nonnegotiable for you. Discuss this with your attorney in advance of any mediation or negotiation sessions so that he or she can support you in focusing the discussions on the issues you are open to looking at.

6.12 What is the role of my attorney in the mediation process?

The role of your attorney in the mediation process will vary depending upon your situation. Your attorney can assist you in identifying which issues will be discussed in mediation and which are better left to negotiation or to the judge. Your attorney can suggest strategies and advise you as to your strengths and weaknesses regarding various issues.

In all cases it is important that your attorney review any agreements discussed in mediation before a final agreement is reached.

6.13 How do I prepare for mediation?

Prior to attending a mediation session with your spouse, discuss with your attorney the issues you intend to mediate.

Enlist your attorney's support in identifying your intentions for the mediation. Make a list of the issues most important to you. For example, when it comes to your child, you might consider whether it is your child's safety, the parenting time schedule, or the ability to attend your children's events that concerns you most.

Be forward looking. Giving thought to your desired outcomes while approaching mediation with an open mind and heart is the best way to move closer to settlement. Also think about what is important to your spouse. That way you may be able to craft an argument or proposal that appeals to him or her, and not merely an argument or proposal that makes you "the winner."

6.14 Do children attend the mediation sessions?

Like any part of the process, children are not included except under extremely rare circumstances. Their presence would only create more anxiety for everyone.

6.15   I want my attorney to look over the agreements my spouse and I discussed in mediation before I give my final approval. Is this possible?

Yes. Usually, the mediator will tell you to have your attorney review all agreements with you. Before giving your written or final approval to any agreements reached in mediation, it is critical that your attorney review the agreements first. This is necessary to ensure that you understand the terms of the settlement and its implications. Your attorney will also review the agreement for compliance with New York law.

6.16   Who pays for mediation?

The cost of mediation must be paid for by you or your spouse. Often it is a shared expense. Expect your mediator to address the matter of fees before or at your first session.

6.17   What if mediation fails?

If mediation is not successful, you still may be able to settle your case through negotiations between the attorneys. Also, you and your spouse can agree to preserve the issues for which settlement was reached and take only the remaining disputed issues to the judge for trial.

In mediation, the parties might agree to, say, the amount of life insurance that one party needs to keep in force, but they can't agree as to who gets the antique car. The mediator can prepare an agreement that memorializes the life insurance agreement yet preserves each party's right to dispute the disposition of the car.

6.18   What is a *settlement conference?*

A *settlement conference* is often called a *four-way* and it can be a powerful tool for the resolution of your case. It is a meeting held with at least four people present—you, your spouse, and both lawyers. The intention of the meeting is to negotiate the terms of your divorce. In some cases, a professional with important information needed to support the settlement process, such as an accountant, may also participate.

Settlement conferences are most effective when both parties and their attorneys see the potential for a negotiated resolution and have the necessary information to accomplish that goal.

6.19 Why should I consider a settlement conference when the attorneys can negotiate through letters and phone calls?

A settlement conference can eliminate the delays that often occur when negotiation takes place through correspondence and calls between the attorneys. Rather than waiting days or weeks for a response, you can receive a response on a proposal in a matter of minutes.

A settlement conference also enables you and your spouse, if you choose, to use your own words to explain the reasoning behind your requests. You are also able to provide information immediately to expedite the process.

6.20 How do I prepare for my settlement conference?

Being well prepared for the settlement conference can help you make the most of this opportunity to resolve your case without the need to go to trial. Actions you should take include:

- Provide in advance of the conference all necessary information. If your attorney has asked for a current pay stub, tax return, debt amounts, asset values, or other documentation, make sure it is provided prior to the meeting.

- Discuss your topics of concern with your attorney in advance. Your lawyer can assist you in understanding your rights under the law so that you can have realistic expectations for the outcome of negotiations.

- Bring a positive attitude, a listening ear, and an open mind. Come with the attitude that your case will settle. Be willing to first listen to the opposing party, and then to share your position. To encourage your spouse to listen to your position, listen to hers or his first. Resist the urge to interrupt.

Few cases settle without each side demonstrating flexibility and a willingness to compromise. Most cases settle when the parties are able to bring these qualities to the process.

6.21   What will happen at my settlement conference?

Typically, the conference will be held at the office of one of the attorneys, with both parties and lawyers present. If there are a number of issues to be discussed, an agenda may be used to keep the focus on relevant topics. From time to time throughout the conference, you and your attorney may meet alone to consult as needed. If additional information is needed to reach agreement, some issues may be set aside for later discussion.

The length of the conference depends upon the number of issues to be resolved, the complexity of the issues, and the willingness of the parties and lawyers to communicate effectively. An effort is made to confirm which issues are resolved and which issues remain disputed. Then, one by one the issues are addressed.

6.22   What is the role of my attorney in the settlement conference?

Your attorney is your advisor and advocate during the settlement conference. You can count on him or her to support you throughout the process, to see that important issues are addressed, and to counsel you privately outside the presence of your spouse and his or her lawyer.

6.23   Why is my lawyer appearing so friendly with my spouse and her lawyer?

Successful negotiations rely upon building trust between the parties working toward agreement. Both lawyers should be respectful and courteous toward you, toward your spouse, and toward each other to promote a good outcome.

6.24   What happens if my spouse and I settled some but not all of the issues in our divorce?

You and your spouse can agree to maintain the agreements you have reached and let the judge decide those matters that you are unable to resolve.

6.25   If my spouse and I reach an agreement, how long will it take before we are divorced?

If a settlement is reached through negotiation or mediation, one of the attorneys will put the agreement in writing for approval by you and your spouse. Once the agreement is signed, it is often the case that no court appearance is required. A number of documents can be prepared and signed. Then these documents are submitted to the court as an uncontested motion. A judge will sign a judgment of divorce in a relatively short time after the documents are submitted.

7

Emergency:
When You Fear Your Spouse

Suddenly, you are in a panic. Maybe your spouse was serious when he or she threatened to take your child and leave the state. What if you're forced out of your own home? Suppose all of the bank accounts are emptied? Your fear heightens as your mind spins with all of the possibilities from every horror story you ever heard about divorce.

Facing an emergency situation in divorce can feel as though your entire life is at stake. You may not be able to concentrate on anything else. At the same time, you may be paralyzed with anxiety and have no idea how to begin to protect yourself. No doubt you have countless worries about what your future holds.

When facing an emergency, do your best to focus on what to do in the immediate moment.

7.1   My spouse has deserted me. What is my first step?
Your first step is to get legal advice as soon as possible. The earlier you get legal counsel to advise you about your rights, the better. The initial consultation will answer most of your questions and start you on an action plan.

7.2   I'm afraid my abusive spouse will try to hurt me and/ or our children if I say I want a divorce. What can I do legally to protect myself and my children?
You need to develop a plan with your safety and that of your children as your highest priority. Your risk of harm from an abusive spouse increases when you leave. For this reason, all actions must be taken with safety as the first concern.

73

Find a lawyer who understands domestic violence. A local domestic violence agency may help with a referral. Talk to your lawyer about the concerns for your safety and that of your children. Ask your lawyer about "orders of protection." These are court orders that may offer a number of protections including ordering your spouse to leave the family residence and have no contact with you. Orders of protection are powerful tools—a violation of an order can result in the immediate arrest of your spouse.

7.3   I am afraid to meet with a lawyer because I am terrified my spouse will find out and get violent. What should I do?
Schedule an initial consultation with an attorney who is experienced in working with domestic violence victims. When you schedule the appointment, let the firm know your situation and instruct the law office not to place any calls or send e-mails or text messages to you that your spouse might discover.

Consultations with your attorney are privileged. Your lawyer has an ethical duty to not disclose your meeting with anyone outside of the law firm. Let your attorney know your concerns so that extra precautions can be taken by the law office in handling your file.

7.4   I want to give my attorney all the information needed so my children and I are safe from my spouse. What does this include?
Provide your attorney with complete information about the history, background, nature, and evidence of your abuse including:

*   The types of abuse (for example, physical, sexual, verbal, financial, mental, emotional)
*   The dates, time frames, or occasions
*   The locations
*   Whether you were ever treated medically
*   Any police reports made
*   E-mails, letters, notes, or journal entries
*   Any photographs taken

- Any witnesses to the abuse or evidence of the abuse
- Any statements made by your spouse admitting the abuse
- Any damaged property
- Injuries you or your children suffered
- Any counseling you had because of the abuse
- Alcohol or drug abuse
- The presence of guns or other weapons

The better the information you provide to your lawyer, the easier it will be for him or her to make a strong case for the protection of you and your children.

7.5 I'm not ready to hire a lawyer for a divorce, but I am afraid my spouse is going to get violent with my children and me in the meantime. What can I do?

It is possible to seek a protection order from the court without an attorney. It is possible for the judge to order your spouse out of your home and to stay away from you and the children.

7.6 What's the difference between an order of protection and a civil restraining order?

Both orders of protection and *civil restraining orders* are court orders that direct a person to not engage in certain behavior. Both of them are intended to protect others. Both can initially be obtained without notice to the other person although there is always a right to a hearing to determine whether a protection order or restraining order should remain in place. The main difference, and it's a big difference, is that the violation of an order of protection can be handled immediately by the police—they can arrest your spouse. A violation of the restraining order is a civil matter, handled through your attorney, who can make an application to hold your spouse in contempt. This involves a hearing before a judge that may not occur for months.

7.7 My spouse has never been violent, but I know she is going to be really angry and upset when the divorce papers are served. Can I get an order of protection?

The facts of your case may not convince a judge to issue an order of protection. However, if you are still concerned about your spouse's behavior, ask your attorney about a *temporary restraining order (TRO)* to be delivered to your spouse at the same time as the divorce complaint. This court order could direct your spouse not to annoy, threaten, intimidate, or harass you while the divorce is in progress.

7.8 My spouse says I am crazy, that I am a liar, and that no judge will ever believe me if I tell the truth about the abusive behavior. What can I do if I don't have any proof?

Most domestic violence is not witnessed by third parties. Often there is little physical evidence. Even without physical evidence, a judge can enter orders to protect you and your children if you give truthful testimony about abuse the judge finds it believable. Your own testimony of your abuse is evidence. There may be more evidence than you think. Perhaps there are text messages, e-mails, or voice-mail messages that can give a judge some insight into the dynamics of your relationship with your spouse.

It is very common for persons who abuse others to claim that their victims are liars and to make statements intended to discourage disclosure of the abuse. This is yet another form of controlling behavior.

Your attorney's skills and experience will support you to give effective testimony in the courtroom to establish your case. Let your lawyer know your concerns so that a strong case can be presented to the judge based upon your persuasive statements of the truth of your experience.

7.9 I'm afraid my spouse is going to take all of the money out of the bank accounts and leave me with nothing. What can I do?

Talk to your attorney immediately. If you are worried about your spouse emptying financial accounts or selling marital assets, it is critical that you take action at once. Your attorney can advise you on your right to take possession of certain assets in order to protect them from being hidden or spent by your spouse.

Ask your lawyer about triggering *automatic orders*, which go into effect immediately. These orders direct that neither you nor your spouse can sell, transfer, hide, or otherwise dispose of property until the divorce is complete or until a court orders otherwise. Additionally, these orders prevent a host of other types of chicanery.

7.10 My spouse told me that if I ever file for divorce, I'll never see my child again. Should I be worried about my child being abducted?

Your fear that your spouse will abduct your children is a common one. It can be helpful to look at some of the factors that appear to increase the risk that your child will be removed from the state by the other parent.

Does your spouse have a prior criminal record? Are his or her social or economic ties to the community limited? Does he or she have family in another country? Have there been efforts to isolate the child? Has your spouse been inordinately interested in the status of a passport? Has she or he been getting financial matters in order?

Talk to your lawyer to assess the risks in your particular case. Together you can determine whether statements by your spouse are threats intended to control or intimidate you or whether legal action is needed to protect your child.

7.11 What legal steps can be taken to prevent my spouse from removing our child from the state?

If you are concerned about your child being removed from the state, talk to your lawyer about whether any of these options might be available in your case:

- A court order giving you immediate custody until a temporary custody hearing can be held
- A court order directing your spouse to turn over passports for the child and your spouse to the court
- The posting of a bond prior to your spouse exercising parenting time
- Supervised visitation

Both state and federal laws are designed to provide protection from the removal of children from one state to another when a custody matter is brought to court, to protect children from kidnapping. *The Uniform Child Custody Jurisdiction and Enforcement Act (UCCJEA)* was passed to encourage the custody of children to be decided in the state where they have been living most recently and where they have the most ties. *The Parental Kidnapping Prevention Act (PKPA)* makes it a federal crime for a parent to kidnap a child in violation of a valid custody order.

If you are concerned about your child being abducted, talk with your lawyer about all options available to you for your child's protection.

7.12 How quickly can I get a divorce in New York?

The answer to this question varies case by case and county by county. Once you have met the residency requirements, the speed with which your case can be concluded depends on whether you need to have a judge determine some issues or all of them. Generally, a divorce will not be granted until all issues have been determined. This can take days or years. Once a judge signs the judgment of divorce, it is effective as of that moment. There are no additional waiting periods.

7.13 I really need a divorce quickly. Will the divorce I get in another country be valid in New York?

Unless that other country has the right to exercise jurisdiction over your spouse, the answer is most likely not. Further, if you have children and they have not resided in that country for at least six months, that country's child-custody determination will most likely not be recognized.

7.14 If either my spouse or I file for divorce, will I be ordered out of my home? Who decides who gets to live in the house while we go through the divorce?

If you and your spouse cannot reach agreement regarding which of you will leave the residence during the divorce, the judge can decide whether one of you should be granted exclusive possession of the home until the case is concluded. Without some extraordinary circumstances, such as showing that remaining together in the home is a danger to you or your children, it is doubtful that either of you will be ordered to leave the home.

8

Child Custody

Ever since you and your spouse began talking about divorce, your children have probably been your greatest concern. You or your spouse might have postponed the decision to seek divorce because of concern about the impact on your children. Now that the time has come, you might still have doubts about whether your children will be all right after the divorce.

It can be difficult not to worry about how the sharing of parenting time with your spouse will affect your children. You may also have fears about being cut out of your child's life. Try to remember that regardless of who has custody, it is likely that the court order will not only give you a lot of time with your children but also a generous opportunity to be involved in their day-to-day lives.

With the help of your lawyer, you can make sound decisions regarding the custody arrangement that is in the best interests of your children.

8.1   What types of custody are awarded in New York?

Under New York law, there are two aspects to a custody determination. These are *legal custody* and *physical custody*. *Legal custody* refers to the power to make important decisions regarding your children. Legal custody may be awarded to you, to your spouse, to both of you jointly, or there may be some areas of decisions granted to you and others to your spouse. For example, you may be the one to decide education and religious matters while your spouse determines medical and extracurricular activity issues.

If you receive sole legal custody, you will be the primary and final decision maker for significant matters regarding your children, such as which school they attend, who are their health care providers, and whether they go to therapy. The noncustodial parent will have parenting time and other rights.

Joint legal custody means that you and your former spouse will share equally in making major decisions for your child. If you and the other parent are unable to reach agreement, you may need to enlist the help of a third party. That could be a mediator, a parent coordinator, or a judge.

Joint legal custody is strongly encouraged if:

- There has been and will continue to be effective and open communication between the parents concerning the child.

- There is a strong desire on the part of both parents to continue to co-parent together.

- There is a history of active involvement of both parents in the child's life.

- There are similar parenting values held by both parents.

- There appears to be a willingness on the part of both parents to place the child's needs before their own.

- Both parents are willing to be flexible and compromising about making decisions concerning the child.

It is rare that a court will impose joint legal custody on parents if they do not agree to it.

Physical custody refers to the physical location of the children, that is, where they spend their time. There are many variations of physical custody arrangements. Some parents try to have a true 50/50 sharing of time, like a week with one parent followed by a week with the other. Or one parent gets Monday and Tuesday, the other Wednesday and Thursday, and weekends alternate. Other parents are more comfortable with a less than equal schedule. It really depends on what is best for the children given their ages; what is best for you considering your availability, strengths, and weaknesses; and what can actually be accomplished after considering where you and your spouse will live after the divorce. Parenting time does affect support and that is addressed in the next chapter.

8.2   On what basis will the judge award custody?

A judge is directed to make a custody award that is in "the best interests of the child." To determine a child's best interests, the judge looks at the entirety of factors affecting the child. The following is by no means an exhaustive list, but it gives you some idea as to the broad scope of the analysis and why custody trials can be long and expensive:

Home Environments. This refers to the respective environments offered by you and your spouse. The court may consider factors such as the safety, stability, and nurturing found in each home.

Emotional Ties. The emotional relationship between your child and each parent may include the nature of the bond between the parent and child and the feelings shared between the child and each parent.

Age, Sex, and Health of the Child and Parents. New York no longer ascribes to the "tender years" doctrine, which formerly gave a preference for custody of very young children to the mother. If one of the parents has an illness that may impair the ability to parent, it may be considered by the court. Similarly, the judge may look at special health needs of a child.

Effect on the Child of Continuing or Disrupting an Existing Relationship. This factor might be applied in your case if you stayed at home for a period of years to care for your child, and awarding custody to the other parent would disrupt your relationship with your child.

Attitude and Stability of Each Parent's Character. The court will consider your ability and willingness to be cooperative with the other parent and to protect the child's relationship with the other parent in deciding who should be awarded custody. The court may also consider each parent's history, which reflects the stability of his or her character.

Moral Fitness of Each Parent, Including Sexual Conduct. The extent to which a judge assesses the morals of a parent can vary greatly from judge to judge. Sexual conduct will ordinarily not be considered unless it has harmed your child or your child was exposed to sexual conduct.

Child Custody

Capacity to Provide Physical Care and Satisfy Educational Needs. Here the court may examine whether you or the other parent is more focused on your child's daily needs such as nutrition, health care, hygiene, social activities, and education. The court may also look to see whether you or your spouse have been attending to these needs in the past.

Preferences of the Child. The child's preference regarding custody will be considered if the child is of sufficient age of comprehension, regardless of chronological age, and the child's preference is based on sound reasoning. New York does not allow a child to choose the parent he or she wishes to live with. Rather, at any age the court may consider the well-reasoned preferences of a child. Typically, the older the child, the greater the weight given to the preference. However, the child's reasoning is also important. New York does provide for a judge to appoint an attorney for the child. This attorney represents the child just like your attorney represents you. If you have more than one child, each child may get his or her own attorney if it is determined that each child's position is different from the other.

Health, Welfare, and Social Behavior of the Child. Every child is unique. Your child's needs must be considered when it comes to deciding custody and parenting time. The custody of a child with special needs, for example, may be awarded to the parent who is better able to meet those needs.

The judge may also consider whether you or your spouse has fulfilled the role of primary care provider for meeting the day-to-day needs of your child.

Domestic Violence. Domestic violence is an important factor in determining legal custody, as well as parenting time and protection from abuse during the transfer of your child to the other parent. If domestic violence is a concern in your case, be sure to discuss it in detail with your attorney during the initial consultation so that every measure can be taken to protect the safety of you and your children.

8.3 What's the difference between *visitation* and *parenting time?*

Historically, time spent with the noncustodial parent was referred to as *visitation*. Today, the term *parenting time* is used to refer to the time a child spends with either parent.

This change in language reflects the intention that children spend time with both parents and have two homes, as opposed to their living with one parent and visiting the other.

8.4 How can I make sure I will get to keep the children during the divorce proceedings?

A court order is the best way to be sure your children will stay with you while your divorce is proceeding. Even if you and your spouse have agreed to temporary arrangements, talk with your attorney about whether this agreement should be formalized in a court order so that it can be enforced.

Obtaining a temporary order (referred to as a *pendente lite order)* can be an important protection not only for the custody of your children, but for other issues such as support and temporary exclusive possession of the marital home, payment of counsel fees, and a host of other matters that need to be stabilized as you proceed through the divorce process.

Until a *pendente lite* order is entered, it's best that you continue to reside with your children if obtaining custody of them is important to you. It is usually recommended that the children stay in the family home. If you think you must leave your home, talk with your attorney about taking the children with you and seeking the appropriate court orders.

8.5 How much weight does the child's preference carry?

The preference of your child is only one of many factors a judge considers in determining custody. The older the child, the more weight is given to the child's preference. But knowing the child's "preferences" does not end the inquiry. The reasoning underlying the preference is very important. Consider the fifteen-year-old girl who wants to live with her mother because "Mom lets me stay out past curfew, I get a bigger allowance, and I don't have to do chores." Greater weight might be given to the preference of an eight-year-old who wants to live with his mother because "she helps me with my homework, reads me bedtime stories, and doesn't call me names like Dad does."

If you see that your child's preference may be a factor in the determination of custody, discuss this with your lawyer so that it is taken into consideration when assessing the action to be taken in your case.

8.6 How can I prove that I was the primary care provider?

One tool to assist you and your attorney in establishing your case as a primary care provider is a Parental Roles Chart indicating the care you and your spouse have each provided for your child. The clearer you are about the history of parenting, the better job your attorney can do in presenting your case to the judge.

Look at the activities in the chart following to help you review the role of you and your spouse as care providers for your child.

Parental Role Chart

Activity	Mother	Father
Attended prenatal medical visits	✓	
Attended prenatal class	✓	✓ first
Took time off work after child was born	✓	✓ week
Got up with child for feedings	✓	
Got up with child when sick at night	✓	
Bathed child	✓	
Put child to sleep	✓	
Potty-trained child	✓	
Prepared and fed meals to child	✓	
Helped child learn numbers, letters, colors, etc.	✓	
Helped child with practice for music, dance lessons, sports	✓	
Took time off work for child's appointments	✓	
Stayed home from work with sick child	✓	
Took child to doctor visits	✓	
Went to pharmacy for child's medication	✓	
Administered child's medication	✓	

Activity	Mother	Father
Took child to therapy		
Took child to optometrist		
Took child to dentist		
Took child to get haircuts		
Bought clothing for child		
Bought school supplies for child		
Transported child to school		
Picked up child after school		
Drove carpool for child's school		
Went to child's school activities		
Helped child with homework and projects		
Attended parent–teacher conferences		
Helped in child's classroom		
Chaperoned child's school trips and activities		
Transported child to child care		
Communicated with child-care providers		
Transported child from child care		
Attended child-care activities		
Signed child up for sports, dance, music		
Bought equipment for sports, dance, music		
Transported child to sports, dance, music		
Attended sports, music, dance practices		
Coached child's sports		
Transported child from sports, dance, music		
Knows child's friends and friends' families		
Took child to religious education		
Participated in child's religious education		
Obtained information and training about special needs of child		
Comforted child during times of emotional upset		

8.7   Do I have to let my spouse see the children before we are actually divorced?

Unless your children are at risk for being harmed by your spouse, your children should maintain regular contact with the other parent.

It is important for children to experience the presence of both parents in their lives, regardless of the separation of the parents. Even if there is no temporary order for parenting time, cooperate with your spouse in making reasonable arrangements for time with your children.

When safety is not an issue, if you deny contact with the other parent prior to trial, your judge is likely to question whether you have the best interests of your child at heart. Talk to your spouse or your lawyer about what parenting time schedule would be best for your children on a temporary basis.

8.8   I am seeing a therapist. Will that hurt my chances of getting custody?

If you are seeing a therapist, commend yourself for getting the professional support you need. Your well-being is important to your ability to be the best parent you can be.

Talk over with your lawyer the implications of your being treated by a therapist. It may be that the condition for which you are being treated in no way affects your child or your ability to be a loving and supportive parent.

Your mental health records may be subpoenaed by the other parent's lawyer. For this reason it is important to discuss with your attorney an action plan for responding to a request to obtain records in your therapist's file. Ask your attorney to contact your therapist to alert him or her regarding how to respond to a request for your mental health records.

8.9   Can having a live-in partner hurt my chances of getting custody?

If you are contemplating having your partner live with you, discuss your decision with your attorney first. If you are already living with your partner, let your attorney know right away so that the potential impact on any custody ruling can be assessed.

Your living with someone who is not your spouse may have significant impact on your custody case. However, judges' opinions of the significance of this factor can vary greatly. Talk promptly and frankly with your lawyer. It will be important for you to look together at many aspects, including the following:

- How the judge assigned to your case views this situation

- Whether your living arrangement is likely to prompt a custody dispute that would otherwise not arise

- How long you have been separated from the other parent

- How long you have been in a relationship with your new partner

- The history and nature of the children's relationship with your partner

- Your future plans with your partner (such as marriage)

Think carefully about your decision to have your partner live with you, taking into consideration the advice of your lawyer.

8.10 Will all the sordid details of my or my spouse's affair have to come out in court in front of our children?

A threshold question must first be answered: What impact does the affair have when viewed through the prism of your children's best interests? If it has no relevance, it may not be part of the court proceeding.

However, if it's relevant, judges make every effort to protect children from the conflict of their parents. Children are usually not present in the courtroom to hear the testimony of other witnesses.

Although the risk that your spouse may share information with your child cannot be eliminated, it would be highly unusual for a judge to allow a child to hear such testimony in a courtroom.

Child Custody

8.11 Should I hire a private detective to prove my spouse is having an affair?

It depends. If custody is disputed and your spouse is having an affair, discuss with your attorney how a private investigator might help you gather evidence to support your case. Discuss the following considerations with your attorney:

- What view on extramarital relationships does my judge hold?
- How is the affair affecting the children?
- How much will a private investigator cost?
- Will the evidence gathered help my case?

Your attorney can help you determine whether hiring a private investigator is a good idea in your particular case.

8.12 Will the fact that I had an affair during the marriage hurt my chances of getting custody?

In this day and age, the mere fact of an affair is not likely, in and of itself, to have an impact. Whether a past affair will have any impact on your custody case will depend upon a few factors, including:

- The views of the judge assigned to your case
- Whether the affair had any impact on the children
- How long ago the affair occurred
- The quality of the evidence about the affair

If you had an affair during your marriage, discuss it with your attorney at the outset so that you can discuss its impact, if any, on custody.

8.13 During the months it takes to get a divorce, is it okay to date or will it hurt my chances at custody?

If custody is disputed, talk with your attorney about your plans to begin dating. Your dating may be irrelevant if the children are unaware of it. However, some judges frown upon exposing your children to a new relationship when they are still adjusting to the separation of their parents.

If your spouse is contesting custody, you may see that it would be best to focus your energy on your children, the litigation, and taking care of yourself.

If you do date and become sexually involved with your new partner, it is imperative that your children not be exposed to any sexual activity. If they are, it could harm your case for custody.

8.14 I'm gay and came out to my spouse when I filed for divorce. What impact will my sexual orientation have on my case for custody or parenting time?

New York has been on the vanguard of the parenting rights and marriage rights of gay people. It should have little impact, in and of itself.

Although exposing your child to sexual activity or engaging in sexual activity that harms your child are relevant factors in a custody dispute, your choice of a same-sex or opposite-sex sexual partner does not change the analysis. That said, you are certainly aware that not everyone has gotten in step with same-sex relationships, and that includes your spouse, lawyers, or judges who have not yet dispelled certain myths. Try to select a lawyer who will fully support you.

8.15 How is *abandonment* legally defined, and how might it affect the outcome of our custody battle?

Abandonment is rarely an issue in custody litigation unless one parent has been *completely* absent from the child's life for an extended period. After being absent, a parent is at risk of having his or rights terminated. It is a drastic step and will not be taken lightly, and will only be done if it would be in the best interests of the child.

8.16 Can I have witnesses speak on my behalf to try to get custody of my children?

Absolutely. Witnesses are critical in every custody case. In connection with an application for a *pendente lite* order, a witness is more likely to provide testimony by affidavit, which is a written, sworn statement. However, at a trial for the final determination of custody, you and the other parent will each have an opportunity to have witnesses give live testimony on your behalf.

Among those you might consider as potential witnesses in your custody case are:

- Family members
- Family friends
- Child-care providers
- Neighbors
- Teachers
- Health care providers
- Clergy members

In considering which witnesses would best support your case, your attorney may consider the following:

- What opportunity has this witness had to observe you or the other parent, especially with your child. How frequently? How recently?
- How long has the witness known you or the other parent?
- What is the relationship of the witness to the child and the parents?
- How valuable is the knowledge that this witness has?
- Does this witness have knowledge different from that of other witnesses?
- Is the witness available and willing to testify?
- Is the witness clear in conveying information?
- Is the witness credible, that is, will the judge believe this witness?
- Does the witness have any biases or prejudices that could impact the testimony?

You and your attorney can work together to determine which witnesses will best support your case. Support your attorney by providing a list of potential witnesses together with your opinion regarding the answers to the above questions.

Give your attorney the phone numbers, addresses, and workplaces of each of your potential witnesses. This information can be critical for the role that the attorney has in interviewing the witnesses, contacting them regarding testifying, and issuing subpoenas to compel their court attendance if needed. When parents give conflicting testimony during a custody trial, the testimony of other witnesses can be key to determining the outcome of the case.

8.17 How old do the children have to be before they can speak to the judge about whom they want to live with?

It depends upon the judge. There is no set age at which children are allowed to speak to the judge about their preferences as to custody.

If either you or your spouse want to have the judge listen to what your child has to say, a request is ordinarily made to the judge to have the child speak to the judge in the judge's office (chambers) rather than from the witness stand. Depending upon the judge's decision, the attorneys for you and your spouse may also be present, or perhaps just the judge and the child's attorney. The child's statement to the judge will be recorded and the transcript sealed.

It is possible that the judge may also allow the attorneys to submit questions for the child.

Typically, the testimony of the child is made "on the record," that is, in the presence of a court reporter. This is so that the testimony can be transcribed later in the event of an appeal.

In addition to the age of a child, a judge may consider such facts as the child's maturity and personality in determining whether an interview of the child by the judge will be helpful to the custody decision-making process. This is referred to as an *in camera* interview, or a *Lincoln Henry.*

8.18 Will my attorney want to speak with my children?

No.

8.19 What is a guardian *ad litem*? Why is one appointed?

In some custody cases, a guardian *ad litem* is an individual who is appointed by the court to represent the best interests a child who is too young to have an attorney. The guardian *ad litem* (sometimes referred to as "the GAL"), typically a mental health professional, conducts an investigation on the issue of custody.

The guardian *ad litem* may be called as a witness by you or your spouse to give testimony of her or his knowledge, based upon the investigation. For example, he or she might testify regarding the unsafe housing conditions of a parent or the ability of one parent to better care for the child.

8.20 What's a *forensic evaluator*?

In many cases a judge will appoint a psychologist or psychiatrist to conduct an investigation into the parenting abilities of you and your spouse. The investigation may involve psychological testing, drug and alcohol testing, and extensive interviews and document reviews. The *forensic evaluator* will interact with you and your spouse separately and will also often observe you with your children and your spouse with your children. These observations may occur at your home, at the office of the evaluator, or perhaps elsewhere. The evaluator will ordinarily provide the court with a report of each party's strengths and weaknesses as a parent, the presence or absence of substance abuse, the presence of mental illness, and the like. The judge will then consider all these facts in making the custody determinations.

8.21 How might a videotape or DVD of my child help my custody case?

A staged, scripted, or edited video will likely have little value and will not be admitted into evidence.

Talk to your lawyer about whether a videotape would be helpful in your case. Such a video could show routines in your child's day, including challenging moments such as bedtime or disciplining.

If your lawyer recommends making a videotape, talk with him or her about what scenes to include, the length of the video, keeping the original tapes, and the editing process.

8.22 Why might I not be awarded custody?

You will not be awarded custody if the judge determines that you are not fit to be a custodial parent or that the other parent is "more fit." Determinations of your fitness to be a custodial parent and of the best interests of your child will largely depend upon the facts of your case. Reasons why a parent might be found to be unfit include a history of physical abuse, alcohol or drug abuse, or mental health problems that affect the ability to parent. A judge's ruling on the best interests of a child is based upon numerous factors.

A decision by the judge that your spouse should have custody does not require a conclusion that you are an unfit parent. Even if the judge determines that both you and your spouse are fit to have custody, he or she may nevertheless decide that it is in the best interests of your child that only one of you be awarded custody.

8.23 Does joint custody always mean equal time at each parent's house?

No. Joint *legal custody* (equal decision-making authority) does not necessarily mean joint *physical custody* (equal division of parenting time).

Whether you or your spouse have sole legal or joint legal custody, you and your spouse can agree to share parenting time in a way that best serves your children. An example would be where you and your spouse agree to joint legal custody, but where you will be the primary physical custodian, with your child spending more time with you than with your spouse. It can also be helpful to remember that day-to-day decisions, such as a child's daily routine, will usually be made by the parent who has the child that day.

8.24 What are some of the risks of joint legal custody?

Joint legal custody may be a good idea when the parents agree to it, they have been separated for a period of time and have been able to reach decisions regarding their children without the involvement of attorneys or the court, and where the other factors for joint legal custody are present.

Joint legal custody requires healthy communication between you and your spouse. Without it, you are at risk for conflict, stress, and delay when making important decisions for your child. If communication with your spouse regarding your child is poor, think carefully before agreeing to joint legal custody.

If you share joint legal custody and are unable to reach agreement on a major decision, such as a child's school or child-care provider, you and your former spouse may be required

Child Custody

to return to court to resolve your dispute or find some other way to break the impasse. This can lead to delays in decision making for matters important to your child, increased conflict, and legal fees.

8.25 If my spouse is awarded primary physical custody of our child, how much time will our child spend with me?

There is no magical formula for parenting time. The schedules vary from case to case. As in the determination of legal custody, the best interests of the child are what a court considers in determining the parenting time schedule.

Among the factors that can impact a parenting time schedule are the past history of parenting time, the age and needs of the child, and the parents' work schedules.

If you and your spouse are willing to reach your own agreement about the parenting time schedule, you are likely to be more satisfied with it than with one imposed by a judge. Because the two of you know your child's needs, your family traditions, and your personal preferences, you can design a plan uniquely suited to your child's best interests.

If you and your spouse are unable to reach an agreement on a parenting time schedule, either on your own or with the assistance of your lawyers, the judge will decide the schedule.

8.26 What is a parenting plan?

A *parenting plan* is a document that details how you and your spouse will be parenting your child after the divorce. Among the issues addressed in a parenting plan are:

- Custody, both legal and physical
- Parenting time, including specific times for:
    * Regular school year
    * Holidays
    * Birthdays
    * Mother's Day and Father's Day
    * Summer
    * School breaks
- Phone access to the child

- Communication regarding the child
- Access to records regarding the child
- Notice regarding parenting time
- Attendance at the child's activities
- Decision making regarding the child
- Exchange of information such as addresses, phone numbers, and care providers

You can see a sample parenting plan template at: www.nycourts.gov/forms/matrimonial/parentingplanform.pdf.

8.27   I don't think it's safe for my children to have any contact with my spouse. How can I prove this to the judge?

Keeping your children safe is so important that this discussion with your attorney requires immediate attention. It will most likely involve the appointment of an attorney for your children or a GAL and a mental health forensic evaluator. Talk with your attorney about a plan for the protection of you and your children. Options might include an order of protection, supervised parenting time, random drug or alcohol testing, or other restrictions on your spouse's parenting time.

Make sure you have an attorney who understands your concerns for the welfare of your children. If your attorney is not taking your worry about the safety of your children seriously, you may be better served by a lawyer with a greater understanding of the issues in your case.

Give your attorney a complete history of the facts upon which you base your belief that your children are not safe with the other parent. Although the most recent facts are often the most relevant, it is important that your attorney have a clear picture of the background as well.

Your attorney also needs information about your spouse, such as whether your spouse is or has been:

- Using alcohol or drugs
- Treated for alcohol or drug use
- Arrested, charged, or convicted of crimes of violence
- In possession of firearms
- Subject to a protection order for harassment or violence

8.28 My spouse keeps saying he'll get custody because there were no witnesses to his abuse and I can't prove it. Is he right?

No. Most domestic violence is not witnessed by others, and judges know this. If you have been a victim of abusive behavior by your spouse, or if you have witnessed your children as victims, your testimony is likely to be the most compelling evidence. Think about the availability of text messages, e-mails, or voice-mail messages as well.

Be sure to tell your attorney about anyone who may have either seen your spouse's behavior or spoken to you or your children right after an abusive incident. They may be important witnesses in your custody case.

8.29 I am concerned about protecting my child from abuse by my spouse. Which types of past abuse by my spouse are important to tell my attorney?

Keeping your child safe is your top priority. So that your attorney can help you protect your child, give him or her a full history of the following:

- Hitting, kicking, pushing, shoving, or slapping you or your child
- Sexual abuse
- Threats of harm to you or the child
- Threats to abduct your child
- Destruction of property
- Torture or other harm to pets
- Requiring your child to keep secrets

The process of writing down past events may help you to remember other incidents of abuse that you had forgotten. Be as complete as possible.

8.30   What documents or objects should I give my attorney to help prove the history of domestic violence by my spouse?

The following may be useful exhibits if your case goes to court:

- Photographs of injuries
- Photographs of damaged property
- Abusive or threatening notes, letters, or e-mails
- Abusive or threatening voice-mail messages
- Your journal entries about abuse
- Police reports
- Medical records
- Court records
- Criminal and traffic records
- Damaged property, such as torn clothing

Discuss with your attorney any of these items that you are able to obtain and ask your lawyer whether others can be acquired through a subpoena or other means.

8.31   Under what circumstances will a court direct supervised parenting time?

If you are concerned about the safety of your children when they are with the other parent, talk to your lawyer. It may be that an order of protection is warranted to terminate or limit your spouse's contact with your children. Alternatively, it is possible to ask the judge to consider certain court orders intended to better protect your children.

Ask your attorney whether, under the facts of your case, the judge would consider any of the following court orders:

- Supervised time
- Exchanges of the children in a public place/police station
- Parenting classes
- Anger management or other rehabilitative program for the other parent

- A prohibition against drinking by the other parent when with the children

Judges have differing approaches to cases where children are at risk. Recognize that there are also often practical considerations, such as cost or the availability of people to supervise visits. Urge your attorney to advocate zealously for court orders to protect your children from harm by the other parent.

8.32 I want to talk to my spouse about our child, but all she wants to do is argue. How can I communicate without it always turning into a fight?

If conflict is high between you and your spouse, consider the following:

- A court order for custody and parenting time that is specific and detailed lowers the amount of necessary communication between you and your spouse.

- Put as much information in writing as possible. Consider using e-mail, mail, or fax, especially for less urgent communication. This not only assures that there is record of your involving the other parent, but it gives the other parent time to respond, and not just give a knee-jerk response.

- Avoid criticisms of your spouse's parenting.

- Perhaps try to schedule a conversation with your spouse in advance, with a planned agenda, so no one feels ambushed.

- Avoid directing your spouse regarding how to parent.

- Be factual, concise, and businesslike.

- Acknowledge to your spouse the good parental qualities he or she displays, such as being concerned, attentive, or generous.

- Keep your child out of any conflicts.

By focusing on your behavior, conflict with your spouse has the potential to decrease.

8.33 What if the child is not returned from parenting time at the agreed-upon time? Should I call the police?

Calling the police should be done only if you feel that your child is being abused or neglected, some crime is being committed, or if you have been advised by your attorney that such a call is warranted. The failure to return a child as scheduled is normally not a crime.

The appropriate response to a child not being returned according to a court order depends upon the circumstances. If the problem is a recurring one, talk to your attorney regarding your options. It may be that a change in the schedule would be in the best interests of your child.

Regardless of the behavior of the other parent, make every effort to keep your child out of any conflicts between the adults.

8.34 Can I relocate with my child without the consent of the other parent?

Usually not. If the relocation will affect the other parent's parenting time or role with regard to legal custody, you will be required to get a court order permitting the move (whether to a different county, state, or country). If your former spouse agrees to your move, contact your attorney for preparing and submitting the necessary documents to your former spouse and to the court for approval.

If your former spouse objects to your move, you must apply to the court for permission, give your spouse notice of the application, and have a court hearing for the judge to decide.

To obtain the court's permission, you must prove that the move is in the best interests of your child. Temporary removal of a child in such cases is ordinarily not granted. It may be important to expedite your case so you will have a final court ruling determining whether you may move with your child.

8.35   What factors does the court consider when determining the best interests of the child when considering relocation?

As with custody, the determination of your child's best interests involves more factors than can be listed and depends heavily on the circumstances of your particular situation. If you're merely considering a move, talk to your attorney immediately. Do so even if you have not finalized your plans. There are important facts for you to gather as soon as possible.

8.36   After the divorce, can my spouse legally take our children out of the state during parenting time? Out of the country?

It depends upon the terms of the court order as set forth in your decree. If you are concerned about your children being out of New York with the other parent, discuss the possibility of some of these provisions regarding out-of-state travel with your child:

- Limits on the duration or distance for out-of-state travel with the child
- Notice requirements, such as having the traveling parent provide the nontraveling parent with some advance notice of the plans (perhaps forty-five or sixty days)
- Information on phone numbers
- Information on physical addresses
- E-mail address contact information
- Restrictions with regard to possession of the child's passport
- Posting of bond by the other parent prior to travel
- Requiring a court order for travel outside of the country

Although judges are not ordinarily concerned about short trips across state lines, you should let your attorney know if you are concerned that your child may be abducted by the other parent so that reasonable safeguards may be put in place.

8.37   If I am not given custody, what rights do I have regarding medical records and medical treatment for my child?

Regardless of which parent has custody, both parents have the right to access to the medical records of their children and to make emergency medical decisions.

8.38   If I'm not the primary caregiver, how will I know what's going on at my child's school? What rights to records do I have there?

Regardless of your custodial status, you have a right to access to your child's school records.

Develop a relationship with your child's teachers and the school staff. Request to be put on the school's mailing list for all notices. Find out what is necessary for you to get copies of important school information and report cards.

Communicate with the other parent to both share and receive information about your child's progress in school. This will enable you to support your child and each other through any challenging periods of your child's education. It also enables you to share a mutual pride in your child's successes.

Regardless of which parent has custody, your child will benefit by your involvement in his or her education by your participation in parent-teacher conferences, attendance at school events, help with school homework, and positive communication with the other parent.

8.39   What if my child does not want to go for his or her parenting time? Can my former spouse force the child to go?

If your child is resisting going with the other parent, it can first be helpful to determine the underlying reason. Consider these questions:

- What is your child's stated reason for not wanting to go?
- Does your child appear afraid, anxious, or sad?
- Do you have any concerns regarding your child's safety while with the other parent?
- Have you prepared your child for being with the other

parent, speaking about the experience with enthusiasm and encouragement?

- Is it possible your child is perceiving your anxiety about the situation and is consequently having the same reaction?

- Have you provided support for your child's transition to the other home, such as completing fun activities in your home well in advance of the other parent's starting time for parenting?

- Have you spoken to the other parent about your child's behavior?

- Can you provide anything that will make your child's time with the other parent more comfortable, such as a favorite toy or blanket?

- Have you established clear routines that support your child to be ready to go with the other parent with ease, such as packing a backpack or saying good-bye to a family pet?

The reason for a child's reluctance to go with the other parent may be as simple as being sad about leaving you or as serious as being a victim of abuse in the other parent's home. It is important to look at this situation closely to determine the best response.

Judges treat compliance with court orders for parenting time seriously. If one parent believes that the other is intentionally interfering with parenting time or the parent-child relationship, it can result in further litigation and the loss of legal and physical custody rights. At the same time, you want to know that your child is safe. Talk with your attorney about the best approach in your situation.

8.40 What steps can I take to prevent my spouse from getting custody of the children in the event of my death?

Unless the other parent is not fit to have custody, he or she will have first priority as the guardian of your child in the event of your death. For a third party to obtain custody involves custody litigation in which your surviving spouse begins with a significant advantage. Nonetheless, if this is a concern, seek counsel about how to best document and preserve the evidence that will be needed to prove that the other parent is unfit to have custody in the event of your death.

9

Child Support

Whether you will be paying child support or receiving it, child support payments are often the subject of much worry. Will I receive enough support to take care of my children? Will I have enough money to live on after I pay my child support? How will I make ends meet?

All parents presumably want to provide for their children. Today, the child-support laws make it possible for parents to have a better understanding of their obligation to support their children. The mechanisms for both payment and receipt of child support are more clearly defined, and help is available for collecting support if it's not paid.

The *Child Support Standards Act (CSSA)* helps to simplify the child-support system. As you learn more about the standards, matters regarding child support that appear complex in the beginning can eventually become routine for you and the other parent.

9.1   What determines whether I will get child support?

Whether you will receive child support depends upon a couple of factors. First, are you the primary custodial parent? Second, is the income of the other parent sufficiently above the "self-support" level? If the answer to both these questions is "yes," then you receive child support from the other parent.

If you and your spouse are still living together, providing for the support of the children becomes a bit more complicated.

9.2   Can I request child support even if I do not meet the residency requirements for a divorce in New York?

Yes. Even though you may not have met the residency requirements to obtain a divorce, you have a right to seek support for your children. Talk to your attorney.

9.3   Can I get temporary support while waiting for custody to be decided?

A judge has authority to enter a temporary order for custody and child support. This order ordinarily remains in place until a final decree establishing custody is entered.

In most cases the issues of temporary custody and support can be determined shortly after the proceeding has begun.

9.4   How do I get temporary child support?

If an agreement between spouses is not reached, it is likely that your attorney will file a motion for temporary child support, asking the judge to decide how much the support should be and when it will start.

Because there are a number of steps to getting a temporary child-support order, don't delay in discussing your need for support with your lawyer. Child support will not be ordered for any period prior to the filing of a request for it with the court.

The following are the common steps in the process:

- You discuss your need for a temporary child-support order with your lawyer.
- Necessary financial information is gathered and organized.
- Your sworn statement of net worth is prepared.
- A motion is made.
- Your spouse responds.
- You reply.
- A court appearance occurs.
- The temporary order is prepared by the judge, either at the court appearance or up to sixty days later, (sometimes even longer.)
- Hopefully, your spouse obeys the order and pays you voluntarily.

Child Support

If your spouse does not pay you support voluntarily, you will need to pursue enforcement of the order, which can take more time.

9.5   How soon does my spouse have to start paying child support?

If you are entitled to receive child support, your spouse may begin paying you support voluntarily at any time. A temporary order for support gives you the right to collect the support if your spouse stops paying. Talk to your lawyer about the time it will take to get a *pendente lite* child-support order; it could take months.

9.6   Whether I will receive child support or pay it, how is the amount of "ultimate" child support figured?

The Child Support Standards Act (CSSA) was created by New York legislation to set forth a uniform method for the calculation of child support. That does not mean that parties in Poughkeepsie, New York, will have the same amount of support set as parties in New York City. According to the guidelines, both parents have a duty to contribute to the support of their children in proportion to their respective net incomes. As a result, both your income and the income of your spouse will factor into the child-support calculation. However, the calculation is not strictly formulaic. The formula is not required to be applied to income over a certain amount. Currently, the amount is $136,000 and consists of combined parental income subject to the formula. However, this number gets adjusted every year. Furthermore, the judge has a great amount of discretion to deviate from the guidelines, but with the courts being so understaffed, it is not easy to get a judge to set aside the time necessary to make a determination. Some factors that may lead a judge to deviate from the formula are:

- Whether the noncustodial parent incurs extraordinary expenses in order to spend time with the child.
- Whether either parent or child has extraordinary medical costs
- Whether a child is disabled with special needs

- Whether the application of the guidelines in an individual case would be unjust or inappropriate.

You can review the guidelines in greater detail at: www.nycourts.gov/divorce/childsupport.

9.7 Will the type of custody arrangement or the amount of parenting time I have impact the amount of child support I receive?

Generally, no. The formula does not have a provision for an adjustment based on the amount of time that the main custodial parent spends with the children. In fact, court decisions have made it clear that in a situation in which each parent shares time with the children equally, the party with the higher income pays child support to the party with the lower income.

9.8 Is overtime pay or a bonus considered in the calculation of child support?

Yes, if your overtime is a regular part of your employment and you can expect to earn it regularly, or if you historically receive a bonus, then the judge can consider your work history, the degree of control you have over your overtime, and the nature of the field in which you work.

9.9 Will other income be factored into my child support, or just my salary?

Income from all other sources will be considered in determining the amount of child support. Worker's compensation, disability payments, unemployment benefits, Social Security, veteran's benefits, pensions, fellowships, annuities, the income that could be generated by non-income-providing assets, employment "perks" that are really for personal use or otherwise reduce personal expenses, the value of fringe benefits, and money from friends or relatives are all considered. Further, if a court finds someone intentionally reduced his or her income in order to lower support, the court can make a support order based on what the court thinks that person should be earning.

Child Support

9.10 My spouse has a college degree but refuses to get a job. Will the court consider this in determining the amount of child support?

The earning capacity of your spouse may be considered instead of current income. The court can look at your spouse's work history, education, skills, health, and job opportunities.

If you believe your spouse is earning substantially less than the income she or he is capable of earning, provide your attorney with details. Ask about making a case for child support based on earning capacity instead of actual income. In order for the judge to determine someone's true earning capacity, there will need to be expert testimony submitted.

9.11 Will I get the child support directly from my spouse or from the state?

You can insist that the child support be paid to the state's *Support Collection Services (SCU),* in which case your payment will come from the SCU if the other parent pays. If the other parent fails to pay, the SCU will commence enforcement processings and perhaps obtain an income-deduction order. You should speak with your attorney about the pluses and minuses of utilizing support collection services.

You may want to visit the Division of Child Support Enforcement at www.childsupport.ny.gov/dcse/home.

9.12 If my spouse sends in a child-support payment to the SCU, how quickly will the state mail me a check?

A number of factors affect how quickly your child-support payment will be paid to you after it is received by the SCU, such as whether it is a payment by cashier's check, electronic funds transfer, or credit card. The SCU does not accept personal checks.

9.13 Is there any reason not to pay or receive payments directly to or from my spouse once the court has entered a child-support order?

Yes. Once a child-support order is entered by the court, the SCU can keep a record of all support paid. If the payment is not made through the SCU, its records will not show if your spouse is behind in child support. The SCU will calculate any cost of living adjustments to which you may be entitled. They will help you locate the other parent if he or she "disappears" and stops paying. Finally, the SCU can invoke a host of administrative remedies to enforce the payment obligation such as attachment of paychecks, intercepting refunds, seizing assets, reporting delinquencies to the credit agencies, and suspending driving and other licenses.

Direct payments of child support from your spouse can also result in misunderstandings between parents. The payer may have intended the money to pay a child-support payment, but the parent receiving the support may have thought it was extra money to help with the child's expenses. Sometimes a payment may be in cash and the receipt or the cash can be "forgotten."

The payment of support through the SCU protects both parents.

9.14 Can I go to the courthouse to pick up my child-support payment?
No.

9.15 How soon can I expect my child-support payments to start arriving?
A number of factors may affect the date on which you will begin receiving your child support. Here are the usual steps in the process:

- A child-support amount and start date for the support are decided either by agreement between you and your spouse or by the judge.

- If the judge does not write the order, then either your attorney or your spouse's attorney prepares the court order.

- The attorney who did not write the court order reviews and approves it.

- The court order is then taken to the judge for signature. If you are using the SCU you go to the SCU and complete the paperwork.

- The child support is then paid to the SCU.

- The SCU sends the money to you.

Child Support

As you can see, there are a lot of steps in this process. Plan your budget knowing that the initial payment of child support might be delayed.

9.16 If my spouse has income other than from an employer, is it still possible to get a direction to withhold my child support from his income?

Yes. If you are eligible for an income attachment, child support can be automatically withheld from many sources of income.

9.17 The person I am divorcing is neither the biological nor adoptive parent of my child. Can I still collect child support from my spouse?

Perhaps. Discuss the facts of your case with your lawyer in detail. When you are clear about what will be in the best interests of your child, your attorney can support you in developing a strategy for your case that takes into consideration not only child support but also the future relationship of your spouse with your child.

9.18 Can I collect child support from both the biological parent and the adoptive parent of my child?

No. When your child was adopted, the biological parent's duty to support your child ended. If, however, there was an order to support that directed the biological parent to pay support and you were due to receive money by virtue of that order before the adoption, then that debt is still owed to you and you have the right to collect it.

9.19 What happens with child support when our children go to other parent's home for summer vacation? Is child support still due?

Unless you agree otherwise, the answer is "yes." Basic child support is essentially used to provide food, clothing, and shelter to the children. The only expense that is reduced when they are not with you is food. The court often provides for a reduction in child support if a child lives away from home to go to boarding school or college.

9.20 After the divorce, if I choose to live with my new partner rather than marry, can I still collect child support?

Yes. Although spousal maintenance may end if you live with your partner, child support does not terminate for this reason.

9.21 Can I still collect child support if I move to another state?

Yes. A move out of state will not end your right to receive child support. However, the amount of child support could be changed if other circumstances change, such as income or costs for exercising parenting time. Relocating with a child brings up many issues. A careful consideration of all these issues should be made with a knowledgeable attorney before attempting to move.

9.22 Can I expect to continue to receive child support if I remarry?

Yes. Your child support will continue even if you remarry.

9.23 How long can I expect to receive child support?

Under New York law, child support is ordered to be paid until the child is emancipated or reaches the age of twenty-one. The determination of what constitutes "emancipation" is not a simple one and, once again, you should discuss your specific circumstances with your counsel.

9.24 Does interest accrue on past-due child support?

Unless otherwise set out in an agreement, the court can order interest to be charged on past due support.

9.25 What can I do if my former spouse refuses to pay child support?

If your former spouse is not paying child support, you may take action to enforce the court order either with the help of your lawyer or the assistance of the SCU.

The judge may order payment of both the current amount of support and an additional amount to be paid each month until the past due child support (referred to as "arrearages") is paid in full.

You may get a judgment for the arrearages and attach it to the other parent's paycheck, including income from other sources, bank accounts, brokerage accounts, life insurance, cash values, virtually anything of value including a home, boat, car, and so on.

Driver's licenses may also be suspended if a parent falls behind in child-support payments.

Your former spouse may also be found in contempt of court if the failure to pay support is judged to be "willful." A possible consequence of being found in contempt is a jail sentence. In certain circumstances, failure to pay child support is a criminal offense and can be prosecuted by the district attorney. This is not a common occurrence.

9.26 I live outside New York. Will the money I spend on airline tickets to see my children impact my child support?

It might. If you expect to spend large sums of money for transportation in order to have parenting time with your children, talk to your attorney about how this might be taken into consideration when determining the amount of child support.

9.27 After the divorce, can my former spouse substitute buying sprees with the child for child-support payments?

No. Purchases of gifts and clothing for a child do not relieve your former spouse from an obligation to pay you child support.

9.28 Are expenses such as child care supposed to be taken out of my child support?

No. Child-care expenses are separate from child support because the court recognizes that child care for young children is often a tremendous expense. Therefore, the guidelines provide that each parent pay a percentage of the work- or school-related child-care expenses in addition to the child support.

Other expenses for your child such as clothing, school lunches, and the cost for some activities are ordinarily paid for by you if you are receiving child support according to the guidelines, unless the court order in your case provides otherwise.

9.29 Can my spouse be required by the divorce decree to pay for our child's private elementary and high school education?

Yes, under the proper circumstances. In the larger cities of New York, private schools (at both the elementary and secondary school levels) are a common and large expense. Your attorney can evaluate your particular circumstances and advise you as to the likelihood of obtaining a court order directing a contribution for private schooling.

9.30 Can my spouse be required by the decree to contribute financially to our child's college education?

Your attorney can evaluate your particular circumstances and advise you as to the likelihood of obtaining a court order directing a contribution for a college education. The amount of the contribution will be affected by the unique circumstances of your family including the current age of your child, your financial situation, and the educational needs of the child.

If your agreement or judgment is to include a provision for payment of college education expenses, be sure it is as specific as possible. Specific items to consider include:

- What expenses are included? For example, tuition, room and board, books, fees, travel, etc.

- Is there a limit? For example, up to the level of the cost of attendance at a state university of New York or a certain dollar amount.

- When are payments due? Are they to be made to a college savings account between now and the child's matriculation in college?

- Who is the custodian of the account?

- Make sure the custodian is ordered not to use the money for anything except the education of the child.

- For what period of time does it continue?

114

- Are there any limits on the type of education that will be paid for?

The greater the clarity in such a provision, the lower the risk is for misunderstanding or conflict years later.

10

Maintenance and Spousal Support

Maintenance might stir your emotions and start your stomach churning. If your spouse filed for divorce and sought maintenance, you might see it as a double injustice—your marriage is ending and you feel like you have to pay for it, too. If you are seeking spousal support, you might feel hurt and confused if your spouse is resistant to help support you, even though you may have interrupted your career to stay home and care for your children.

Learning more about New York's laws on maintenance, also referred to as *spousal support,* can help you move from your emotional reaction to the reality of possible outcomes in your case. Uncertainty about the precise amount of maintenance that may be awarded or the number of years it might be paid is not unusual. Work closely with your lawyer. Be open to possibilities.

With the help of your lawyer, you will know the best course of action to take toward a decision you can live with after your divorce is over.

10.1 Which gets determined first, child support or maintenance?

Usually, maintenance. Often, once an amount of maintenance is determined, it is subtracted from the payer's income before a child-support calculation is made. After maintenance ends, its dollar amount is added back into the income and a recalculation of child support is done.

10.2 What's the difference between spousal support, alimony, and maintenance?

There is no difference. New York uses the term *maintenance*.

10.3 Are their different types of maintenance?

There is *temporary maintenance,* which can be awarded during the period between the filing of the divorce and the entry of the judgment of divorce. There is *durational maintenance,* which lasts for a fixed period of time after the judgment of divorce. There is *nondurational maintenance,* which terminates only upon the death of either spouse or the recipient spouse's remarriage.

10.4 How will I know if I am eligible to receive maintenance?

Entitlement to temporary maintenance is a matter of a statutory formula that you can find at www.nycourts.gov/divorce under the tab "Temporary Maintenance Tools." The amount calculated by the formula is the amount to which you are "presumably" entitled. You or your spouse can argue that the amount is unjust or inappropriate under the circumstances and a judge will make the ultimate decision. In terms of a post-divorce durational or nondurational maintenance, the court considers many factors that may affect your eligibility such as:

- What is your income and what assets do you own, including your equitable distribution award?
- What is the length of your marriage?
- How old are each of you, and how healthy are you both?
- What are your current and future earning capacities?
- What were your contributions to the marriage, including the interruption of your career?
- Does someone need to go back to school or get retrained?
- Did you live together before you got married?
- How long have you lived apart?
- Did one of you prevent or obstruct the other's career or job, including by the effect of domestic violation?

- What are the ages and needs of any children in your home, including stepchildren and disabled adult children?
- Are there exceptional child-related expenses?
- Is either spouse guilty of wasteful disposition of assets?

Every case for maintenance is unique. Providing your lawyer with clear and detailed information about the facts of your marriage and current situation will increase the likelihood of a fair outcome for you.

As of this writing there are bills pending in the New York legislature that may significantly change both the temporary and post-divorce methods of awarding maintenance. Whether the bills will pass and what the legislation might ultimately provide is impossible to predict. The history in the New York legislature with respect to formulas is that they often have undesired and unintended consequences.

10.5 What information should I provide to my attorney if I want maintenance?

If your attorney advises you that you are a candidate for maintenance, be sure to provide complete facts about your situation, including:

- A history of the interruptions in your education or career for the benefit of your spouse, including transfers or moves due to your spouse's employment
- A history of the interruptions in your education or career for raising children, including periods during which you worked part-time
- Your complete educational background, including the dates of your schooling or training and degrees earned
- Your work history, including the names of your employers, the dates of your employment, your duties, your pay, and the reason you left
- Any pensions or other benefits lost due to the interruption of your career for the benefit of the marriage
- Your health history, including any current diagnoses, treatments, limitations, and medications

- Your monthly living expenses, including anticipated future expenses such as health insurance and tax on maintenance.

- A complete list of the debts for you and your spouse

- Income for you and your spouse, including all sources

Also include any other facts that might support your need for maintenance, such as other contributions you made to the marriage, upcoming medical treatment, or a lack of jobs in the field in which you were formerly employed.

No two cases are alike when it comes to maintenance judgments. The better the information your lawyer has about your situation, the easier it will be for him or her to assess your case for spousal support.

10.6   How is the amount of maintenance calculated?

Under current law, there are no formulas for determining the amount of maintenance to be paid after the judgment of divorce. As mentioned earlier, there are proposals in the legislature to establish a formula for the amount and the duration of postdivorce maintenance. For now, however, a judge will look at all the factors listed previously. In the event a claim for an award of a portion of a spouse's "enhanced earning capacity" is being made, the income used by the judge for the spouse who will be directed to pay maintenance may be significantly less than the actual income. That will be discussed later in Chapter 11. At the current time, judges are given a lot of discretion to make their own decision on maintenance without the benefit of specific guidelines. Consequently, the outcome of a support ruling by a judge can be one of the most unpredictable aspects of your divorce.

10.7   My spouse told me that because I had an affair during the marriage, I have no chance to get maintenance even though I quit my job and have cared for our children for many years. Is it true that I have no case?

That is not the law in New York. Your right to maintenance will be based upon many factors, but having an affair is not a bar to getting spousal support.

10.8   My spouse makes a lot more money than he reports on our tax return, but he hides it. How can I prove my spouse's real income to show he can afford to pay maintenance?

Alert your attorney to your concerns. Your lawyer can then take a number of actions to determine your spouse's income with greater accuracy. This is likely to include:

- More thorough discovery, and perhaps retaining a forensic accountant.
- An examination of check registers and bank deposits
- Reviewing purchases made in cash
- Inquiring about travel
- Depositions of third parties who have knowledge of income or spending by your spouse
- Subpoena of records of places where your spouse has made large purchases or received income
- Comparing income claimed with expenses paid

By partnering with your lawyer, you may be able to build a case to establish your spouse's actual income as greater than is shown on your tax returns. But you must be careful. If you filed joint tax returns with your spouse, discuss with your lawyer the other implications of signing returns with incorrect income or deductions.

10.9   I want to be sure the records on the maintenance I pay are accurate, especially for tax purposes. What's the best way to ensure this?

Pay by personal check or electronic funds transfer. But be sure the check or transfer is only for the amount of maintenance due. Sometimes couples get involved in adjusting payments based on advances or combining child support and maintenance in one payment. Each payment should stand on its own and checks should be exchanged. It appears cumbersome, but it's worth the effort if a disagreement arises.

10.10 How is the purpose of maintenance different from the payment of my property settlement?

Maintenance and the division of property serve two distinct purposes, even though many of the factors for determining them are the same. The purpose of maintenance is to pay for your continued support, whereas the purpose of a property division is to distribute the marital assets acquired during the marriage.

10.11 How long can I expect to receive maintenance?

New York has been moving away from lifetime maintenance awards since the law of equitable distribution was enacted in 1980. Now, lifetime awards are very rare. How long you will receive maintenance will depend upon the other financial dispositions of your case, your prospects of obtaining employment, and the judge's philosophy.

You may receive only temporary maintenance, or you may receive maintenance for several years. Talk to your attorney about the facts of your case to get a clearer picture of the possible outcomes in your situation. Unless you and your spouse agree otherwise, your maintenance will terminate upon your remarriage or the death of either of you. Unless otherwise stated, the payments are included in your income for tax purposes and the payments can be deducted from your spouse's income for tax purposes.

10.12 Does remarriage affect my maintenance?

Yes. Under New York law, maintenance ends upon the receiver's remarriage, unless you and your spouse agree otherwise. For this limited purpose, New York law states you can be "remarried" even if you are merely living together under certain circumstances.

10.13 Can I continue to collect maintenance if I move to a different state?

Yes. The duty of your former spouse to follow a court order to pay maintenance does not end simply because you move to another state.

10.14 What can I do if my spouse stops paying maintenance?

If your spouse stops paying maintenance, see your attorney about your options for enforcing your court order. The judge may order the support taken from a source of your spouse's income or from a financial account belonging to your spouse.

If your spouse is intentionally refusing to pay spousal support, talk to your attorney about whether pursuing a contempt of court action would be effective. In a contempt action, your spouse may be ordered to appear in court and provide evidence explaining why support has not been paid. Possible consequences for contempt of court include a jail sentence or a fine.

10.15 Can I return to court to modify maintenance?

It depends and it's very difficult. If there has been an unforeseeable material change in the circumstances of either you or your spouse and your financial circumstances are dire, you may seek to have maintenance modified.

If you think you have a basis to modify your maintenance award or obligation, contact your attorney at once to be sure a timely modification request is filed with the court.

11

Equitable Distribution of Property

What can be the most confusing and complex aspect of your divorce is the process of equitable distribution. Marital property needs to be identified. Separate property needs to be identified. Valuations need to occur. Each party's contribution needs to be established, and, finally, a fair distribution needs to be determined. This aspect of the case can be expensive and time consuming. Hopefully, what follows will help you decide which fights are worth fighting.

11.1 What system does New York use for dividing property?

New York law provides for an equitable or fair, but not necessarily equal, division of the property and debts acquired during your marriage. Your marriage is deemed to exist between the date of the marriage itself and the date a divorce proceeding was commenced or some other period if you and your spouse agree.

Regardless of how title to any property is held, the court can use its discretion to determine a division of the marital assets. Depending on the nature of the assets and the acts of the parties, the division can be very lopsided.

The court will consider a number of factors, many of which are the same as those used in determining support.

11.2 What does *community property* mean?

Community property is a term used in several states that have a community property system for dividing assets in a divorce. New York is not a community property state. In states having community property laws, each spouse holds a one-half interest in most property acquired during the marriage.

Divorce in New York

11.3 How is it determined who gets the house?

The first issue regarding the family home is often a determination of who will get to live in it while the divorce is pending. Later, it must be decided whether the house will be sold or whether it will be awarded to you or your spouse.

If you and your spouse are unable to reach agreement regarding the house, the judge will decide who keeps it or whether it will be sold. Sometimes a judge will strongly consider whether it's in the children's best interest for them to remain in the home with the custodial parent for some period of time after the divorce.

11.4 Should I sell the house during the divorce proceedings?

In New York you can't sell your house without your spouse's consent. Even if you have sole title, the *automatic orders* will prevent you from selling it.

11.5 What is meant by *equity* in my home?

Regardless of who is awarded your house, the court will consider whether the spouse not receiving the house should be compensated for the equity in the house. By *equity* we mean the difference between the value of the home and the amount owed in mortgages against the property.

For example, if the first mortgage is $50,000 and the second mortgage from a home equity loan is $10,000, the total debt owed "against" the house is $60,000. If your home is valued at $100,000, the equity in your home is $40,000. (The $100,000 value less the $60,000 in mortgages equals $40,000 in equity.) Unless the house is going to be immediately sold, there is no reduction in the value for the costs of selling (like broker's commissions, transfer taxes, and attorney fees), nor is there a reduction for any possible capital gains taxes that could be due.

If one of the parties remains in the home, the issue of how to give the other party his or her share of the equity must be considered. This can provide a good source for creative negotiations that can impact child-support and maintenance obligations.

124

11.6 How will the equity in our house be divided?

If your home is going to be sold, the equity in the home will most likely be divided at the time of the sale, after the costs of the sale have been paid.

If either you or your spouse will be awarded the house, there are a number of options for the other party to be compensated for his or her share of the equity in the marital home. These could include:

- The spouse who does not receive the house receives other assets to compensate for the value of the equity (just remember that equity in the house is, basically, an "after-tax" asset, so any equalization payment should take that into account).

- The person who remains in the home may refinance the home at some future date and pay the other party his or her share of the equity.

- The parties agree that the property be sold at a future date or upon the happening of a certain event—such as the youngest child completing high school or the remarriage of the party keeping the home. The division of the sales proceeds can account for payments toward maintenance, upkeep, and improvements that were paid for by the spouse who continued to live in it.

Because the residence is often among the most valuable asset considered in a divorce, it is important that you and your attorney discuss the details of its disposition. These include:

- Valuation of the property
- Refinancing to remove a party from liability for the mortgage
- The dates on which certain actions should be taken, such as listing the home for sale
- The real estate agent
- Costs of preparing the home for sale
- Making mortgage payments

If you and your spouse do not agree regarding which of you will remain in the home, the court will decide who keeps it or may order the property sold.

11.7 Who keeps all the household goods until the decree is signed?

The court will ordinarily not make any decisions about who keeps the household goods on a temporary basis. Most couples attempt to resolve these issues on their own rather than incur legal fees to dispute household goods kept on a temporary basis.

11.8 How are assets such as cars, boats, and furniture divided, and when does this happen?

In most cases spouses are able to reach their own agreements about how to divide personal property, such as household furnishings and vehicles.

If you and your spouse disagree about how to divide certain items, it would be wise to consider which items are truly valuable to you, financially or otherwise. Perhaps some of them can be easily replaced. Always look to see whether it is a good use of your attorney fees to argue over items of personal property. If a negotiated settlement cannot be reached, the issue of the division of your property will be made by the judge at trial.

11.9 What is meant by a *property inventory* and how detailed should mine be?

A *property inventory* is a listing of the property you own. It may also include a brief description of the property. Discuss with your attorney the level of inventory detail needed to benefit your case.

Factors to consider when creating your inventory may include:

- The extent to which you anticipate you and your spouse will disagree regarding the division of your property
- Whether you anticipate a dispute regarding the value of the property either you or your spouse is retaining
- Whether you will have continued access to the property if a later inventory is needed or whether your spouse will retain control of the property

- Whether you and your spouse are likely to disagree about which items are premarital, inherited, or gifts from someone other than your spouse

In addition to creating an inventory, your attorney may request that you prepare a list of the property that you and your spouse have already divided or a list of the items you want but your spouse has not agreed to give to you.

If you do not have continued access to your property, talk to your attorney about taking photographs or obtaining access to the property to complete your inventory.

11.10 How and when are liquid assets like bank accounts and stocks divided?

In many cases couples will agree to some division of bank accounts equally at the outset of the case. However, this may not be advisable in your case, particularly if there is one large asset (like the house) which may go to one of you and the other party may need all the cash to secure a new home. Discuss with your attorney about how you should keep an accounting of spending money used from a bank account while your divorce is in progress.

Stocks are ordinarily a part of the final agreement for the division of property and debts. If you and your spouse cannot agree on how your investments should be divided, the judge will make the decision at trial.

11.11 How is pet custody determined?

Pet custody is determined on a case-by-case basis. New York law is that a pet is an item of property and is awarded by the court as the judge sees fit. Factors that courts have considered include:

- Who provided care for the pet?
- Who will best be able to meet the pet's needs?
- What is the children's relationship to the pet?

Courts have awarded the pet to one party and given the other party certain rights, such as:

- Specific periods of time to be spent with the pet

- The right to care for the pet when the other person is not able to
- The right to be informed of the pet's health

If it is important to you to be awarded your family pet, discuss the matter with your attorney. It may be possible to reach a pet-care agreement with your spouse that will allow you to share possession and responsibility for your pet.

11.12 How will our property in another state be divided?

For the purposes of dividing your assets, out-of-state property is treated the same as property in New York. Although a New York court cannot create a change in the title to property located in another state, a judge can order your spouse either to turn the property over to you or to sign a deed or other document to transfer title to you. Disobeying such an order could result in the finding of contempt.

11.13 I worked like a dog for years to support my family while my spouse completed an advanced degree. Do I have a right to any of my spouse's future earnings?

Under the current laws of New York, you have right to share in the value of the spouse's ability to earn more money now with the advanced degree. However, in May of 2013, the New York State Law Review Commission issued a report which suggested that this law may be changed as to eliminate this right and satisfy this type of claim by an award of maintenance instead. For now, howeveryour sacrifices, which created a benefit that will only now be enjoyed by your spouse, are considered in terms of the equitable distribution of marital property. Further, your spouse's future income is considered in setting basic child support and your spouse's share of add-on expenses. Most significantly, your spouse's advanced degree, or professional license or practice, or other career attainments, to the extent they increase his or her earning potential, are valued by a highly qualified expert and given a present after-tax value. You can be awarded a portion of that value, paid in a lump sum, or perhaps paid in installments. New York is unique in valuing the "enhanced earning capacity" conferred on someone by virtue of his or her education and licensing. This is one of the most complicated and, at times, perplexing aspects of a divorce matter. If this is an issue in your case, be sure your attorney is comfortable and experienced with matters like this.

11.14 Are all of the assets—such as property, bank accounts, and inheritances—that I had prior to my marriage still going to be mine after the divorce?

It depends. In many cases the court will allow a party to retain an asset brought into the marriage, but the following are questions the court will consider in making its determination:

- Can the premarital asset be clearly traced? For example, if you continue to own a vehicle that you brought into the marriage, it is likely that it will be awarded to you. However, if you brought a vehicle into the marriage, sold it during the marriage, and spent the proceeds, it is less likely that the court will consider awarding you its value.

- Did you keep the property separate and titled in your name, or did you comingle it with marital assets? Premarital assets you kept separate may be more likely to be awarded to you.

- Did you or the other spouse contribute to the increase in the value of the premarital asset, and can the value of that increase be proven? For example, suppose a party owned a home prior to her marriage. After the marriage, the two parties lived in the home, continuing to make mortgage payments and improvements to the home. Depending on the source of funds or efforts made to pay down the mortgage or effect the improvements, the nontitled spouse may be entitled to a share of equity in the home based on its value at the time of the trial or settlement.

11.15 Will I get to keep my engagement ring?

If your engagement ring was given to you prior to your marriage, it will be considered your separate property and is yours to keep.

11.16 Can I keep gifts and inheritances I received during the marriage?

Similar rules apply to gifts and inheritances received during the marriage as apply to premarital assets, that is, assets you owned prior to the marriage.

Gifts from your spouse to you are *not* your separate property so they are part of the marital estate. So that nice watch or earrings you received on that special occasion are not immune from equitable distribution. For gifts received during the marriage from a third party, such as a gift from a parent, the court will need to determine whether the gift was made to one party or to both. Whether you will be entitled to keep assets you inherited will depend largely on whether they can be clearly identified and traced. When dividing the marital estate, the court considers the fact that one spouse is allowed to keep substantial nonmarital assets (such as an inheritance) as a factor when deciding equitable distribution and spousal maintenance. Income that you do or could receive from the inheritance or other separate property is considered by the court in determining spousal maintenance and child support.

The following factors increase the probability that you will be entitled to keep your inheritance:

- It has been kept separate from the marital assets, such as in a separate account.
- It is titled in your name only.
- It can be clearly identified.
- It has not been commingled with marital assets.
- Your spouse has not contributed to its care, operation, or improvement.

It is less likely that you will be awarded your full inheritance if:

- It was commingled with marital assets.
- Its origin cannot be traced.
- You have placed your spouse's name on the title.
- Your spouse has contributed to the increase in the value of the inheritance.

If keeping your inheritance is important to you, talk to your attorney about the information needed to build your case.

11.17 If my spouse and I can't decide who gets what, who decides? Can that person's decision be contested?

If you and your spouse cannot agree on the division of your property, the judge will make the determination after considering the evidence at your trial.

If either party is dissatisfied with the decision reached by the judge, an appeal to a higher court is possible.

11.18 What is a property settlement agreement or stipulation of settlement?

A property settlement agreement and a stipulation of settlement are essentially the same thing. They are written documents that include all of the financial agreements you and your spouse have reached in your divorce along with the child-custody arrangements. This may include the division of property, debts, child support, maintenance, insurance, and attorney fees. You can reach a partial agreement that resolves some issues but leaves others open. However, in New York, you will not receive a divorce until all issues are resolved in some fashion.

The property settlement is usually incorporated into the judgment of divorce (the final court order dissolving your marriage).

11.19 How are the values of property determined?

The value of some assets like bank accounts, which can be easily determined by documents provided by third parties, are usually not disputed. These assets have a value that is not subject to an opinion. The value of other assets, such as homes or personal property, are more likely to be disputed because the value is determined by an opinion as opposed to an objective fact.

You and your spouse can each give your opinion of the value of property you own. You or your spouse may also have certain property appraised by an expert. You and your spouse can agree on a neutral expert, or you can each retain your own expert. In such cases it may be necessary to have the appraiser appear at trial to give testimony regarding the appraisal and the value of the asset. The decision to use a neutral appraiser or valuation expert or to have your own is influenced by many factors and you should discuss this with your attorney.

If you own substantial assets for which the value is likely to be disputed, talk to your attorney early in your case about the benefits and costs of expert witnesses.

11.20 What does *date of valuation* mean?

Because the value of assets can go up or down while a divorce is pending, New York provides that a judge must set a date for an asset to be valued. The date can be the date of the commencement of the action, the date of trial, or somewhere in between. Of course, you and your spouse can agree on the date any particular asset should be valued. As a rule of thumb, things that have a value which depends on the efforts of you or your spouse (like a business) are likely to be valued at the date of commencement. This is so because the beginning of the divorce signals the end of marital partnership. Any increase in the business's value after that point should belong solely to the person who creates it. Similarly, any loss belongs to that person, too.

If an asset's value is mostly determined by market forces (like a house or stock in a publicly traded company), the date of valuation is much closer to the date of trial. This way neither you nor your spouse gets any advantage or suffers any negative consequence of changing market conditions over which you have no control.

11.21 What happens after my spouse and I approve the property settlement agreement? Do we still have to go to court?

If the agreement resolves all the issues, then you usually do not need to return to court. Your case becomes an uncontested matter and a judgment of divorce can be obtained by the submission of a number of routine documents.

Sometimes, however, it is advisable for everyone to go to court and state on the record that the agreement was entered voluntarily, that no one was under any duress, that everyone had ample time to read it and ask their lawyers questions, and be comfortable with their understanding. This procedure is called an *allocution* and it virtually ensures that neither you nor your spouse will be able to back out of the deal.

11.22 What happens to our individual checking and savings accounts during and after the divorce?

Regardless of whose name is on the accounts, bank accounts may be considered marital assets and may be divided by the court. Of course, the funds in some accounts may be needed to pay bills, legal fees, and ongoing expenses. You and your spouse will be fully accountable for every penny you spend, so be sure to keep good records.

11.23 Who gets the interest from certificates of deposit, dividends from stock holdings, and so forth during the divorce proceedings?

Assuming the interest and dividends came from marital property, this income is divided as part of the overall distribution of marital property.

11.24 Do each one of our financial accounts have to be divided in half if we agree to an equal division of our assets?

No. Rather than incurring the administrative challenges and expense of dividing each asset in half, you and your spouse can decide that one of you will take certain assets equal to the value of assets taken by the spouse. If necessary, one of you can agree to make a cash payment to the other to make an equitable division. But you need to be careful because not all values are as simple as they seem. Say, for example, you have 100 shares of stock in Apple in your account and your spouse has 100 shares of stock in hers. The shares are worth $500 apiece. It would seem you each have $50,000 of stock. That may not be so. If you bought your stock at $200 per share and your wife bought hers at $490 per share, her 100 shares are worth much more than yours. The 100 shares purchased at $490 per share are worth $50,000 less the taxes on the $1,000 gain ($500 – $490 = $10 x 100). The 100 shares bought at $200 per share are worth $50,000 less the taxes on the $30,000 gain ($500 – $200 = $300 x 100).

11.25 What factors determine whether I can get at least half of my spouse's business?

It is unlikely you would receive more than one-half the value of the business and, depending on the nature of the business, the likelihood of getting half is not great. If the value of the business is largely the result of your spouse going to work, it is unlikely that you would receive equal value when you don't have to go to work at the business.

Many factors determine whether you will get a share of your spouse's business and in what form you might receive it. Among the factors the court will look at are:

- Whether your spouse owned the business prior to your marriage
- The components of the business's value
- Your role, if any, in operating the business or increasing its value
- If the business requires a professional license
- The overall division of the property and debts

If either of you owns a business, it is important that you work with your attorney early in your case to develop a strategy for valuing the business and making your case for how it should be treated in the division of property and debts.

11.26 My husband and I have owned and run our own business together for many years. Can I be forced out of it?

Deciding what should happen with a family business when divorce occurs can be a challenge. Because of the risk for future conflict between you and your spouse, the value of the business is likely to be substantially decreased if you both remain owners.

In discussing your options with your lawyer, consider the following questions:

- If one spouse retains ownership of the business, are there enough other assets for the other spouse to receive a fair share of the total marital assets?
- Which spouse has the skills and experience to continue running the business?

- What would you do if you weren't working in the business?

- What is the value of the business?

- What is the market for the business if it were to be sold?

- Could you remain an employee of the business for some period of time even if you were not an owner?

You and your spouse know your business best. With the help of your lawyers, you may be able to create a settlement that can satisfy you both. If not, the judge will make the decision for you at trial.

11.27 I suspect my spouse is hiding assets, but I can't prove it. How can I protect myself if I discover later that I was right?

Ask your lawyer to include language in your divorce decree to address your concern. Insist that it include an acknowledgment by your spouse that the agreement was based upon a full and complete disclosure of your spouse's financial condition. Discuss with your lawyer a provision that allows for setting aside the agreement if it is later discovered that assets were hidden.

11.28 My spouse says I'm not entitled to a share of his stock options because he gets to keep them only if he stays employed with his company. What are my rights?

Stock options are often a very valuable asset. They are also one of the most complex issues when dividing assets during a divorce for these, among other, reasons:

- Each company has its own rules about awarding and exercising stock options.

- Complete information is needed from the employer.

- There are different methods for calculating the value of stock options.

- The reasons the options were given can impact the valuation. For example, some are given for future performance.

- There are cost and tax considerations when options are exercised.

Rather than being awarded a portion of the stock options themselves, you may receive a share of the proceeds when the stock options are exercised, and you may be granted the right to have your spouse exercise your share of options when you want to do so.

If either you or your spouse owns stock options, begin discussing this asset with your attorney early in your case to allow sufficient time to settle the issues or to be well prepared for trial.

11.29 What is a prenuptial agreement and how might it affect the property settlement phase of the divorce?

A *prenuptial agreement,* sometimes referred to as a *pre-marital agreement,* is a contract entered into between two people prior to their marriage. It can include provisions as to how spousal support, property division, and debt repayment will be determined upon the occurrence of certain events (such as the onset of a divorce proceeding, a separation, or death). Matters of child custody and child support are generally not addressed in a prenuptial agreement as such provisions would likely be unenforceable. There are provisions that might indirectly affect concerns of child custody and support, such as who gets to stay in the marital residence and what amount of life insurance should be maintained. This is why a matrimonial practitioner should be included in the team you assemble for the preparation of such agreements. Other persons who should be consulted would be your accountant and estate planning advisor.

11.30 Can a prenuptial agreement be contested during the divorce?

Yes. The court may consider many factors in determining whether to uphold your prenuptial agreement. Among them are:

- Whether your agreement was entered into voluntarily
- Whether your agreement was fair and reasonable at the time it was signed
- Whether there was a fraud perpetrated by one party over another

136

- Whether you and your spouse each had your own lawyer
- Whether you and your spouse each had enough time to consider the agreement

If your have a prenuptial agreement, bring a copy of it to the initial consultation with your attorney. Be sure to provide your lawyer with a detailed history of the facts and circumstances surrounding the negotiation and signing of the agreement.

New York law favors the enforcement of prenuptial agreements. These agreements are not often set aside.

11.31 I've heard the old saying "Possession is nine-tenths of the law." Is that true during divorce proceedings?

It can be. Consulting with an attorney before filing for divorce can reduce the risk that assets will be hidden, transferred, or destroyed by your spouse. This is especially important if your spouse has a history of destroying property, incurring substantial debt, or transferring money without your knowledge.

The possible actions you and your attorney can consider together include:

- Placing your family heirlooms or other valuables in a safe location
- Transferring some portion of financial accounts prior to filing for divorce
- Preparing an inventory of the personal property or hiring a third party to prepare the inventory with photos
- Taking photographs or a video of the property
- Obtaining copies of important financial records or statements

Plans to leave the marital home should also be discussed in detail with your attorney so that any actions taken early in your case are consistent with your ultimate goals.

Speak candidly with your lawyer about your concerns so that a plan can be developed that provides a level of protection that is appropriate to your circumstances.

11.32 I'm Jewish and want my husband to cooperate with obtaining a *get*, which is a divorce document under our religion. Can I get a court order for this?

New York has some very specific rules about each party's responsibility to cooperate with the removal of any religious barriers to remarriage, Jewish or otherwise. Discuss this concern with your attorney early on.

11.33 Who will get the frozen embryo of my egg and my spouse's sperm that we have stored at the health clinic?

The terms of your contract with the clinic govern the rights you and your spouse may have to the embryo, so provide a copy of it to your attorney for review.

11.34 Will debts be considered when determining the division of the property?

Yes. The court will consider the marital debts when dividing the property. For example, if you are awarded a car valued at $12,000, but you owe a $10,000 debt on the same vehicle, the court will take that debt into consideration in the overall division of the assets. Similarly, if one spouse agrees to pay substantial marital credit card debt, this obligation may also be considered in the final determination of the division of property and debts and will be considered when determining spousal maintenance and child support.

If your spouse incurred debts that you believe should be his or her sole responsibility, tell your attorney. Some debts may be considered nonmarital and treated separately from other debts incurred during the marriage. For example, if your spouse spent large sums of money on gambling or illegal drugs without your knowledge, you can argue that those debts should be the sole responsibility of your spouse.

11.35 What happens to the property distribution if one of us dies before the divorce proceedings are completed?

Generally, if your spouse dies prior to the day your judgment of divorce is signed, you will be considered married and treated as a surviving spouse under the law.

138

12

Benefits: Insurance, Retirement, and Pensions

During your marriage, you might have taken certain employment benefits for granted. You might not have given much thought each month to having insurance through your spouse's work. When you find yourself in a divorce, suddenly these benefits come to the forefront of your mind.

You might also, even unconsciously, have seen your own employment retirement benefits as belonging to you and not your spouse, referring to "My 401(k)" or "My pension." After all, you are the one who went to work every day to earn it, right?

When you divorce, some benefits arising from your spouse's employment will end, some may continue for a period of time, and others may be divided between you. Retirement funds, in particular, are often one of the valuable marital assets to be divided in a divorce.

Whether the benefits are from your employer or your spouse's, with your attorney's help you will develop a better understanding of which benefits the law considers to be "yours," "mine," and "ours" for continuing or dividing.

12.1 Will my children continue to have health coverage through my spouse's work even though we're divorcing?

If either you or your spouse currently provides health insurance for your children, it is very likely that the court will order the insurance to remain in place for as long as it remains available and support is being paid for your child.

The cost of insurance for the children will be prorated between you and your spouse based on your respective incomes.

12.2 Will I continue to have health insurance through my spouse's work after the divorce?

It depends. If your spouse currently provides health insurance for you, your spouse's health insurance plan may extend your period of coverage for some time after the judgment of divorce is signed. However, most insurance companies refuse to treat a person as a covered spouse beyond the date of the judgment of divorce.

Investigate the cost and availability of continuing on your spouse's employer-provided plans under a federal law known as COBRA. Not all employer insurance plans are subject to COBRA. If your spouse's plan is subject to COBRA, the coverage can be maintained for up to three years. Although the cost of the premium for the insurance is similar to that paid by the employer, you may be surprised at how expensive it is. Try to find out this expense sooner rather than later so that you can evaluate this as an option.

12.3 What is a QMSO?

A *Qualified Medical Support Order (QMSO)* is a court order providing continued group health insurance coverage for a minor child. A QMSO may also enable a parent to obtain other information about the plan, without having to go through the parent who has the coverage. Rather than allowing only the parent with the insurance to be reimbursed for a claim, under a QMSO, a health insurance plan is required to reimburse directly to the parent who actually paid the child's medical expense. This is a fairly important matter because it will prevent any argument about who paid for what and who received the insurance reimbursement.

12.4 How many years must I have been married before I'm eligible to receive a part of my spouse's retirement fund or pension?

There is no minimum time required by law, however the length of time you have been married will determine how much has been accumulated in the fund or pension, which would be subject to distribution. The length of the marriage is also an important factor in determining what your share of that accumulation would be.

12.5 I contributed to my pension plan for ten years before I got married. Will my spouse get half of my entire pension?

No. The court will award your spouse only a portion of your retirement that was acquired during the marriage.

If either you or your spouse made premarital contributions to a pension or retirement plan, be sure to let your attorney know. This is information essential to determine which portion of the retirement plan should be treated as premarital and thus not available for distribution.

12.6 I plan to keep my same job after my divorce. Will my former spouse get half of the money I contribute to my retirement plan after my divorce?

No. Your former spouse has a claim to only the portion of your retirement savings accumulated during the marriage. Talk with your attorney so that the language of the court order ensures protection of your postdivorce retirement contributions.

12.7 Am I still entitled to a share of my spouse's retirement plan benefits even though I never contributed to one during our twenty-five-year marriage?

Yes. Retirement plans are often one of the most valuable assets accumulated during a marriage. Consequently, the judge will consider the retirement plan along with all of the other marital assets and debts when determining a fair division.

12.8 My lawyer says I'm entitled to a share of my spouse's retirement plan benefits. How can I find out how much I get and when I'm eligible to receive it?

More than one factor will determine your rights to collect from your spouse's retirement plan. One factor will be the terms of the court order dividing the retirement benefits. The court order will tell you whether you are entitled to a set dollar amount, a percentage, or a fraction to be determined based upon the length of your marriage and how long your spouse continues working.

Another factor will be the terms of the retirement plan itself. Some provide for lump-sum withdrawals; others issue payments in monthly installments. Review the terms of your court order and contact the plan administrator to obtain the clearest understanding of your rights and benefits. The value of pension plans is usually a matter for expert testimony and you may need to consult with an actuary or other specialist.

12.9 If I am eligible to receive my spouse's retirement benefits, do I have to be sixty-five to collect them?

It depends upon the terms of your spouse's retirement plan. In some cases it is possible to begin receiving your share at the earliest date your spouse is eligible to receive them, regardless of whether he or she elects to do so. Check the terms of your spouse's plan to learn your options.

12.10 What happens if my former spouse is old enough to receive benefits but I'm not?

Ordinarily, you will be eligible to begin receiving your share of the benefits when your former spouse begins his or hers. Depending upon the plan, you may be eligible to receive them sooner.

12.11 Am I entitled to cost-of-living increases on my share of my spouse's retirement plan?

It depends. If your spouse has a retirement plan that includes a provision for a *cost-of-living allowance (COLA),* talk to your lawyer about whether this can be included in the court order dividing the retirement.

12.12 What circumstances might prevent my getting part of my spouse's retirement benefits?

Some pension plans are not subject to division. If you or your spouse are employed by a government agency, talk with your lawyer about how this may affect the property settlement in your case.

12.13 Does the death of my spouse affect the payout of retirement benefits to me or to our children?

It depends upon both the nature of your spouse's retirement plan and the terms of the court order dividing the retirement benefits. If you want to be eligible for survivorship benefits from your spouse's pension, discuss the issue with your attorney before your case is settled or goes to trial. He or she can advise you.

Some plans allow only a surviving spouse or former spouse to be a beneficiary. Others may allow for the naming of an alternate beneficiary, such as your children.

12.14 How can I be sure I'll get my share of my former spouse's retirement benefits when I am entitled to it years from now?

Rather than relying upon your former spouse to pay you a share of a future retirement benefits, your best protection is a court order that provides for the retirement or pension plan administrator to pay the money directly to you. This type of court order is often referred to as a *Qualified Domestic Relations Order (QDRO)* or, in the case of federal retirement plans, a *Court Order Acceptable for Processing (COAP)*. Such orders help ensure that a nonemployee spouse receives his or her share directly from the employee spouse's plan.

Obtaining a QDRO or COAP is a critical step in the divorce process. They can be complex documents, and a number of steps are required to reduce future concerns about enforcement and fully protect your rights. These court orders must comply with numerous technical rules and be approved by the plan administrator, which is often located outside New York. Because this is an area of technical complexity, your attorney and the attorney for your spouse may recommend that an independent service be retained to prepare the QDRO and get the necessary approvals. Often this is much more reliable and cost effective than having the two matrimonial attorneys deal with the task.

Whenever possible, the retirement plan–related court orders should be done at the same time as the judgment of divorce.

12.15 If my former spouse passes on before I do, can I still collect his or her Social Security benefits?

If you were married to your spouse for ten or more years and you have not remarried, you are eligible for benefits whether your spouse is alive or not. Contact your local Social Security Administration office or visit the SSA website at: www.ssa.gov.

12.16 What orders might the court enter regarding life insurance?

The judge may order you or your spouse to maintain a life insurance policy to ensure that future support payments are made. In most cases you will be required to pay for your own life insurance after your divorce, and you should include this as an expense in your monthly budget. Depending on the amount of your life insurance death benefit, you may want to consider placing the policy in an *irrevocable life insurance trust (ILIT)*. This has a number of positive features. First, it keeps the value of the life insurance death benefit out of your taxable estate. Secondly, depending on the trustee, it ensures that someone familiar with handling a possibly large sum of the money is in charge of the funds that secure your children's future.

12.17 Can the court require in the decree that I be the beneficiary of my spouse's insurance policy, as long as the children are minors or indefinitely?

When a court order is entered for life insurance, it is ordinarily for the purposes of ensuring payment of future support and will terminate when the support obligation has ended.

12.18 My spouse is in the military. What are my rights to benefits after the divorce?

As the former spouse of a military member, the types of benefits to which you may be entitled are typically determined by the number of years you were married, the number of years your spouse was in the military while you were married, and whether or not you have remarried. Be sure you obtain accurate information about these dates.

Among the benefits you may be eligible for are:

- A portion of your spouse's military retirement pay
- A survivor benefit in the event of your spouse's death
- Health care or participation in a temporary, transitional health care program
- Use of certain military facilities, such as the commissary

While your divorce is pending, educate yourself about your right to future military benefits so that you can plan for your future with clarity. If your divorce is still pending, contact your base legal office, or for more information visit the website for the branch of the military of which your spouse was a member.

13

Division of Debts

Throughout a marriage, most couples will have disagreements about money from time to time. You might think extra money should be spent on a family vacation, and your spouse might insist it should be saved for your retirement. You might think it's time you finally get a new car, and your spouse thinks you would be fine driving the ten-year-old van for two more years.

If you and your spouse had different philosophies about saving and spending during your marriage, chances are you will have some differing opinions when dividing your debts in divorce. What you both can count on is that New York law provides that, to reach a fair outcome, the payment of debts must also be taken into consideration when dividing the assets from your marriage.

There are steps you can take to ensure the best outcome possible when it comes to dividing your marital debt. These include providing accurate and complete debt information to your lawyer and asking your lawyer to include provisions in your divorce decree to protect you in the future if your spouse refuses to pay his or her share.

Regardless of how the debts from your marriage are divided, know that you will gradually build your independent financial success when making a fresh start after your divorce is final.

13.1   Who is responsible for paying credit card bills and making house payments during the divorce proceedings?

These issues are either resolved in an interim support agreement or by the court in a *pendente lite* order.

13.2   What, if anything, should I be doing with the credit card companies as we go through the divorce?

If possible, it is best to obtain some separate credit prior to the divorce. This will help you establish credit in your own name and help you with necessary purchases following a separation.

Begin by obtaining a copy of your credit report from at least two of the three nationwide consumer reporting companies: Experian, Equifax, or TransUnion. The Fair Credit Reporting Act entitles you a free copy of your credit report from each of these three companies every twelve months.

To order your free annual report online, go to: www.annualcreditreport.com, call toll-free to (877) 322-8228, or complete an Annual Credit Report Request Form and mail it to: Annual Credit Report Request Service, P.O. Box 105283, Atlanta, Georgia 30348-5283. You can print the form from the Federal Trade Commission website at www.ftc.gov/credit.

Your spouse may have incurred debt using your name. This information is important to relay to your attorney. If you and your spouse have joint credit card accounts and if no divorce action has begun, you may want to contact any credit card company to close the account. Do the same if your spouse is an authorized user on any of your accounts. After the divorce action begins, you may be limited by automatic orders.

If you want to maintain credit with a company, ask to have a new account opened in your own name only. Be sure to let your spouse know if you close an account he or she has been using.

13.3   How is credit card debt divided?

Credit card debt will be divided as a part of the overall division of the marital property and debts. Just as in the division of property, the court considers what is equitable, or fair, in your case.

If your spouse has exclusively used a credit card for purposes that did not benefit the family, such as gambling, prostitutes, or otherwise financing an extramarital affair, talk with your attorney.

13.4   Am I responsible for repayment of my spouse's student loans?

It depends. If your spouse incurred student loans prior to the marriage, it is most likely that he or she will be ordered to pay that debt.

If the debt was incurred during the marriage, how the funds were used may have an impact on who is ordered to pay them. For example, if your spouse borrowed $3,000 during the marriage for tuition, it is likely your spouse will be ordered to pay that debt. However, if a $3,000 student loan was taken out by your spouse, but $1,000 of it was used for a family vacation, then the court would be more likely to order the debt repayment be shared.

The court may also consider payment on student loan debt when calculating the amount of child support to be paid.

If you were a joint borrower on your spouse's student loan and your spouse fails to pay the loan, the lender may attempt to collect from you even if your spouse has been ordered to pay the debt.

If either you or your spouse has student loan debt, be sure to give your attorney the complete history regarding the debt and ask about the most likely outcome under the facts of your case.

If you or your spouse came into the marriage with outstanding loans that were paid off during the marriage, you should get the outstanding balance as of the date of marriage and the amount due at the time the divorce began. You may be entitled to a credit for a portion of the amount paid off during the marriage.

13.5   During the divorce proceedings, am I still responsible for debt my spouse continues to accrue?

It depends. In most cases the court will order each of the parties to be responsible for his or her own post-separation debts.

13.6 During the marriage my spouse applied for and received several credit cards without my knowledge. Am I responsible for them?

It depends. The court will consider the overall fairness of the property and debt division when deciding who should pay this debt. If your spouse secretly bought items with the cards and intends to keep those items, it is likely that she or he will be ordered to pay the debt incurred for the purchases.

If, however, you did not know about the applications, but you knew about the cards and benefitted from the credit extended, you may find the debt is counted as *marital* and factored into the overall distribution.

13.7 During our marriage, we paid off thousands of dollars of debt incurred by my spouse before we were married. Will the court take this into consideration when dividing our property and debt?

Yes it will. Depending upon the length of the marriage, the evidence of the debt, and the amount paid, it may be a factor for the judge to consider.

Be sure to let your attorney know if either you or your spouse brought substantial debt into the marriage.

13.8 Regarding debts, what is a *hold-harmless* clause, and why should it be in the divorce decree?

A *hold-harmless* provision or an *indemnification* provision is intended to protect you in the event that your spouse fails to follow a court order or adhere to the terms of an agreement to pay a debt after the divorce is granted. The language typically provides that your spouse shall "indemnify and hold (you) harmless from liability" on the debt.

If you and your spouse have a joint debt and your spouse fails to pay, the creditor may nevertheless attempt to collect from you. As the creditor is not a party to the divorce, the court is without power to change the creditor's rights and can make orders affecting only you and your spouse.

In the event your spouse fails to pay a court-ordered debt and the creditor attempts collection from you, the *hold-harmless* provision in your divorce decree can be used in an effort to insist that payment is made by your former spouse.

These provisions are usually extensive and include a right to receive reimbursement for any reasonable attorney fees you incur defending against a creditor or pursuing the claim against your former spouse.

13.9   My spouse and I have agreed that I will keep our home; why must I refinance the mortgage?

There may be a number of reasons why your spouse is asking you to refinance the mortgage. First, the mortgage company cannot be forced to take your spouse's name off the mortgage note. This means that if you did not make the house payments, the lender could pursue collection against your spouse.

Second, your spouse may not want to wait to receive a share of the home equity. It may be possible for you to borrow additional money at the time of refinancing to pay your spouse his or her share of the equity in the home.

Third, the mortgage on your family home may prevent your spouse from buying a home in the future. The fact that your spouse remains liable on the debt secured by the mortgage is a fact that appears on his or her credit report. Because there remains a risk that your spouse could be pursued for payment of the debt, a second lender may be reluctant to take the risk of extending further credit to your spouse.

13.10   Can I file for bankruptcy while my divorce is pending?

The short answer is "yes." But you should consult with your attorney if you are considering filing for bankruptcy while your divorce is pending. It will be important for you to ask yourself a number of questions, such as:

- Should I file for bankruptcy on my own or with my spouse?
- How will my filing for bankruptcy affect my ability to purchase a home in the future?
- Which debts can be discharged in bankruptcy, and which cannot?
- How will a bankruptcy affect the division of property and debts in the divorce?

- How might a delay in the divorce proceedings due to a bankruptcy impact my case?
- Which form of bankruptcy is best for my situation?

If you use a different attorney for your bankruptcy than you have for your divorce, be sure that each attorney is kept fully informed about the developments in the other case.

13.11 What happens if my spouse files for bankruptcy during our divorce?

Contact your attorney right away. The filing of a bankruptcy while your divorce is pending can have a significant impact on your divorce. Your attorney can advise you whether certain debts are likely to be discharged in the bankruptcy, the delay a bankruptcy may cause to your divorce, and whether bankruptcy is an appropriate option for you. If your spouse files, then you may be the only one for a creditor to pursue for payment of a debt. Your spouse's filing might trigger the need for you to file, too.

13.12 Can I file for divorce while I am in bankruptcy?

Yes, however, you must receive the bankruptcy court's *approval* with respect to certain aspects of the divorce. While in bankruptcy, your property is protected from debt collection by the *automatic stay*. The stay can also prevent the divorce court from dividing property between you and your spouse until you obtain the bankruptcy court's permission to proceed with the divorce.

13.13 What should I do if my former spouse files for bankruptcy after our divorce?

Contact your attorney immediately. If you learn that your former spouse has filed for bankruptcy, you may have certain rights to object to the discharge of any debts your spouse was ordered to pay under your divorce decree. If you fail to take action, it is possible that you will be held responsible for debts your spouse was ordered to pay.

14

Taxes

Nobody likes a surprise letter from the Internal Revenue Service saying he or she owes more taxes. When your divorce is over, you want to be sure that you don't later discover you owe taxes you weren't expecting to pay.

A number of tax issues may arise in your divorce. Your attorney may not be able to answer all of your tax questions, so consulting your accountant or tax advisor for additional advice might be necessary.

Taxes are important considerations in both settlement negotiations and trial preparation. They should not be overlooked. Taxes can impact many of your decisions including those regarding spousal maintenance, division of property, and the receipt of benefits.

Be sure to ask the professionals helping you about the tax implications in your divorce so you don't get that letter in the mail that begins, "Dear Taxpayer:..."

14.1 Will either my spouse or I have to pay income tax when we transfer property or pay a property settlement to each other according to our divorce decree?

No. However, it is important that you see the future tax consequences of a subsequent withdrawal, sale, or transfer of certain assets you receive in your divorce.

It is important to ask your attorney to take tax consequences into consideration when looking at the division of your assets.

14.2 Is the amount of child support I pay tax deductible?

No.

14.3 Do I have to pay income tax on any child support I receive?

No. Your child support is tax free regardless of when it is paid or when it is received.

14.4 Is the amount of spousal support I am ordered to pay tax deductible?

Unless the divorce judgment says otherwise, yes. Spousal support paid pursuant to a court order is deductible. This will include court-ordered maintenance and may also include other forms of support provided to your former spouse (like payments to third parties but not child support). Your tax deduction is a factor to consider when determining a fair amount of alimony to be paid in your case.

14.5 Do I have to pay tax on the spousal support I receive?

Yes. Unless the court orders otherwise, you must pay income tax on the spousal support you receive. This might also include other forms of spousal support (but not child support) paid by your spouse.

Income tax is a critical factor in determining a fair amount of maintenance. Insist that your attorney bring this issue to the attention of your spouse's lawyer, or to the judge, if your case proceeds to trial, so that both the tax you pay and the deduction your spouse receives are taken into consideration. This could require expert testimony. If you and your spouse are in vastly different tax brackets, the payment of spousal support can be used to effectively increase the amount of money available to your respective households. Say, for example, your spouse is in a 35 percent tax bracket and you are in a 10 percent bracket (That is your spouse pays 35 percent and his or her income in taxes and you pay 10 percent in taxes). Let's further suppose you need $40,000 per year to make your budget. Let's assume your spouse earns $150,000 per year and you make $20,000 per year. One way he or she can pay you is by providing you with $40,000 after-tax dollars, in which case it looks like this:

Spouse	Income	You	Income
	$150,000		$20,000
Less 35 percent	<$52.500>	Less 10 percent	<2,000>
	$97,500		$18,000
Less $40,000	<$40,000>	Plus $40,000	$40,000
Net	$57,000	Net	$58,000

But suppose your spouse pays you $60,000 in deductible/taxable maintenance, which raises you to a 25 percent tax bracket. Then it looks like this:

Spouse	Income	You	Income
	$150,000		$20,000
Less $60,000	<$60,000>	Plus $60,000	$60,000
	$90,000		$80,000
Less Taxes	<$31,500>	Less Taxes	<$20,000>
Net	$58,500	Net	$60,000

Your spouse ends up with an extra $1,000 and you end up with an extra $2,000.

That's $3,500 per year saved for your family.

Be sure to consult with your tax advisor about payment of tax on your spousal support. Making estimated tax payments throughout the year or withholding additional taxes from your wages can avoid a burdensome tax liability at the end of the year.

It is important to budget for payment of tax on your maintenance. Taxes are also another item to consider when looking at your monthly living expenses for the purposes of seeking a maintenance award.

14.6　During the divorce proceedings, is our tax filing status affected?

It can be. You are considered unmarried if your judgment of divorce is final by December 31 of the tax year.

If you are considered unmarried, your filing status is either "single" or, under certain circumstances, "head of household." If your judgment of divorce is not final as of December 31, your filing status is either "married filing a joint return" or "married filing a separate return," unless you live apart from your spouse and meet the exception for "head of household."

While your divorce is in progress, talk to both your tax advisor and your attorney about your filing status. It may be beneficial to figure your tax on both a joint return and a separate return to see which gives you the lower tax. IRS Publication 504, Divorced or Separated Individuals, provides more detail on tax issues while you are going through a divorce.

If possible it is better to cooperate and minimize your joint tax burden than be quarrelsome, which adds attorney fees and increases taxes. However, if you have reason to suspect your spouse is not declaring all income, or is exaggerating deductions, you should steer clear of filing jointly.

14.7 For tax purposes, is one time of year better to divorce than another?

It depends upon your tax situation. If you and your spouse agree that it would be beneficial to file joint tax returns for the year in which you are divorcing, you may wish to not have your divorce finalized before the end of the year.

Your marital status for filing income taxes is determined by your status on December 31. Consequently, if you both want to preserve your right to file a joint return, your judgment of divorce should not be effective until January 1 of the next year.

14.8 What tax consequences should I consider regarding the sale of our home?

When your home is sold, whether during your divorce or after, the sale may be subject to a capital gains tax. If your home was your primary residence and you lived in the home for two of the preceding five years, you may be eligible to exclude up to $250,000 of the gain on the sale of your home. If both you and your spouse meet the ownership and residency tests, you may be eligible to exclude up to $500,000 of the gain.

If you anticipate the gain on the sale of your residence to be more than $250,000, talk with your attorney early in the divorce process about a plan to minimize the tax liability. For more information, see IRS Publication 523, Selling Your Home, or visit the IRS website at www.irs.gov and talk with your tax advisor.

14.9 How might capital gains tax be a problem for me years after the divorce?

Future capital gains tax on the sale of property should be discussed with your attorney during the negotiation and trial preparation stages of your case. This is especially important if the sale of the property is imminent. Failure to do so may result in an unfair outcome. Remember that in New York, both the federal and state governments impose a tax on capital gains. The combined long-term capital gains rate as of this writing is 24 percent.

For example, suppose you agree that your spouse will be awarded the proceeds from the sale of your home valued at $200,000, after the real estate commission, and you will take the stock portfolio also valued at $200,000.

Suppose that after the divorce you decide to sell the stock. It is still valued at $200,000, but you learn that its original price was $120,000 and that you must pay a capital gains tax of 24 percent on the $80,000 of gain. You pay tax of $19,200, leaving you with $180,800.

Meanwhile, your former spouse sells the marital home at $200,000 and pays no capital gains tax because he qualifies for the $250,000 exemption. He is left with the full $200,000.

Tax implications of your property division should always be discussed with your attorney, with support from your tax advisor as needed.

14.10 During and after the divorce, who gets to claim the children as dependents?

This issue should be addressed in settlement negotiations or at trial if settlement is not reached. Everyone should be mindful of who benefits the most from the exemption(s) and how that benefit could be shared. You and your spouse can agree to split the exemptions if you have more than one child or share the exemptions according to an annual schedule.

The judge has discretion to determine which parent will be entitled to claim the children as exemptions for income tax purposes.

If one party has income so low or so high that he or she will not benefit from the dependency exemption, the court may award the exemption to the other parent.

14.11 My judgment of divorce says I have to sign IRS Form 8332 so my former spouse can claim our child as an exemption, because I have custody. Should I sign it once for all future years?

No. Child custody and child support can be modified in the future. If there is a future modification of custody or support, which parent is entitled to claim your child as an exemption could change. The best practice is to provide your former spouse a timely copy of Form 8332 signed by you for the appropriate tax year only.

14.12 Can my spouse and I split the child-care tax credit?

No. Only the custodial parent is allowed to claim the credit. If you are a noncustodial parent and paying for child care, talk to your lawyer about how to address this issue in your settlement agreement.

14.13 Is the cost of getting a divorce, including my attorney fees, tax deductible under any circumstances?

Your legal fees for getting a divorce are not deductible. However, a portion of your attorney fees may be deductible if they are for:

- The collection of sums included in your gross income, such as maintenance or interest income
- Advice regarding the determination of taxes or tax due

Attorney fees are "miscellaneous" deductions for individuals and has certain limits. More details can be found in IRS Publication 529, Miscellaneous Deductions.

You may also be able to deduct fees you pay to appraisers or accountants who help. Talk to your tax advisor about whether any portion of your attorney fees or other expenses from your divorce are deductible.

14.14 Do I have to complete a new Form W-4 for my employer because of my divorce?

Completing a new Form W-4, Employee's Withholding Certificate will help you to claim the proper withholding allowances based upon your marital status and exemptions. Also, if you are receiving maintenance, you may need to make quarterly estimated tax payments. Consult with your tax advisor to ensure you are making the most preferable tax planning decision.

14.15 What is *innocent spouse relief* and how can it help me?

Innocent spouse relief refers to a method of obtaining relief from the Internal Revenue Service for taxes owed as a result of a joint income tax return filed during your marriage. Numerous factors affect your eligibility for innocent spouse tax relief, such as:

- You would suffer a financial hardship if you were required to pay the tax.
- You did not significantly benefit from the unpaid taxes.
- You suffered abuse during your marriage.
- You thought your spouse would pay the taxes on the original return.

Talk with your attorney or your tax advisor if you are concerned about liability for taxes arising from joint tax returns filed during the marriage. You may benefit from a referral to an attorney who specializes in tax law.

15

Going to Court

For many of us, our images of going to court are created by movie scenes and our favorite television shows. We picture the witness breaking down in tears after a grueling cross-examination. We see lawyers waltzing around the courtroom, waving their arms as they plead their case to the jury.

Hollywood drama, however, is a far cry from reality. Going to court for your divorce can mean many things, ranging from sitting in a hallway while waiting for the lawyers and judges conclude a conference to being on the witness stand giving mundane answers to questions about your monthly living expenses.

Regardless of the nature of your court proceeding, going to court often evokes a sense of anxiety. Perhaps your divorce might be the first time in your life that you have even been in a courtroom. Be assured that these feelings of nervousness and uncertainty are normal.

Understanding what will occur in court and being well prepared for any court hearings will relieve much of your stress. Knowing the order of events, the role of the people in the courtroom, proper courtroom etiquette, and what is expected of you will make the entire experience easier.

Your lawyer will be with you at all times to support you any time you go to court. Remember, every court appearance moves you one step closer to completing your divorce so that you can move forward with your life.

15.1 What do I need to know about appearing in court and court dates in general?

Court dates are important. As soon as you receive a notice from your attorney about a court date in your case, confirm whether your attendance will be required and put the date on your calendar.

Ask your attorney about the nature of the appearance. Is it a conference or a hearing? Will the judge will be listening to testimony by witnesses, reading affidavits, or merely listening to the arguments of the lawyers?

Ask whether it is necessary for you to meet with your attorney or take any other action to prepare for the hearing, such as providing additional information or documents.

Find out how long the hearing is expected to last. It may be as short as a few minutes or as long as a day or more.

If you plan to attend the hearing, determine where and when to meet your attorney. Depending upon the type of hearing, your lawyer may want you to arrive in advance of the scheduled hearing time to prepare.

Make sure you know the location of the courthouse, where to park (or if taking mass transit the appropriate stop to take), and the floor and room number of the courtroom. Planning for such simple matters as having change for a parking meter can eliminate unnecessary stress. If you want someone to go to court with you to provide support, check with your attorney first.

15.2 When and how often will I need to go to court?

Whether and how often you will need to go to court depends upon a number of factors. Depending upon the complexity of your case, you may have only one appearance or numerous court appearances throughout the course of your divorce.

Although you are generally required to be at all court appearances, the actual time spent with the judge is often brief and held in the judge's chambers rather than in the courtroom.

If you and your spouse settle all of the issues in your case, there may be no need for a court appearance—ever.

If your case proceeds to trial, your appearance will be needed for the duration of the trial. Although, technically, your appearance is not "required" (unless you have been subpoenaed) it would send a pretty poor message for you not to show up at your own trial. In New York, divorce matters are heard before a judge only. The only chance for a jury trial is if the issue of "fault" is contested. That is where someone wants a divorce based on the other spouse's misconduct (such as extreme cruelty, abandonment, adultery) and the spouse charged with the misconduct demands a trial by jury. This is a very rare event given that New York has a "no-fault" divorce option, jury trials cost a phenomenal amount of money in terms of attorney fees, and the outcome of the jury trial will not significantly affect the other financial issues.

15.3   How much notice will I get about appearing in court?

The amount of notice you will get for any court appearance can vary from a few days (in the case of an emergency) to several weeks or months.

It is unlikely that you would receive a notice from the court directly if you are represented by an attorney. But, if you receive a notice of a hearing, contact your attorney immediately. He or she can tell you whether your appearance is required and what other steps are needed to prepare.

15.4   I am afraid to be alone in the same room with my spouse. When I go to court, is this going to happen if the lawyers go into the judge's chambers to discuss the case?

Talk to your lawyer. Prior to any court appearance, you and your spouse may be asked to wait while your attorneys meet with the judge to discuss preliminary matters.

A number of options are likely to be available to ensure that you feel safe. These might include having you or your spouse wait in different locations or having a friend or family member present. You may want to wait in the courtroom where a court officer is usually present.

Your lawyer wants to support you in feeling secure throughout all court proceedings. Just let him or her know your concerns.

15.5   Do I have to go to court every time there is a court hearing on any motion?

Generally, yes.

15.6   My spouse's lawyer keeps asking for continuances of court dates. Is there anything I can do to stop this?

Adjournments of court dates are not unusual. A court date might be postponed many reasons, including a conflict on the calendar of one of the attorneys or the judge, the lack of availability of one of the parties or an important witness, or the need for more time to prepare. You need to be careful about objecting to the other side's request for an adjournment. You don't want to appear to be unreasonable and there may come a time when you or your attorney needs to reschedule a court date.

15.7   If I have to go to court, will I be put on the stand? Will there be a jury?

Whether you will testify depends upon the nature of the issues in dispute, the judge assigned to your case, and your attorney's strategy for your case. Generally, you will testify at an evidentiary hearing concerning any contested issue in your case. You are the one with the largest repository or knowledge so it is only logical that you will tell your version of the facts. Your lawyer will spend significant time with you in advance to discuss and prepare your direct testimony and to prepare you for the likely areas upon which you will be cross-examined.

15.8   Are there any rules about courtroom etiquette that I need to know?

Knowing a few tips about being in the courtroom will make your experience easier.

- Dress appropriately. Avoid overly casual dress, lots of jewelry, revealing clothing, and extreme hairstyles.
- Don't bring beverages into the courtroom. Most courts have rules that do not allow food and drink in courtrooms. If you need water, ask your lawyer.
- Dispose of chewing gum before giving testimony.

- Don't talk aloud in the courtroom unless you're on the witness stand or being questioned by the judge.
- Do not enter the judge's chambers.
- Remember that the judge is looking at you all the time. Don't make faces, smirk, overly emote, or try to be dramatic.
- Stand up whenever the judge is entering or leaving the courtroom.
- Be sure to turn off your cell phone and pager.

Although you may feel anxious initially, you'll likely feel more relaxed about the courtroom setting once your hearing gets underway.

15.9 What is the role of the court officer and the part clerk?

The *court officer* provides support and security for the judge while the *part clerk* provides support for the judge and lawyers in the management of the court calendar and the courtroom. The part clerk assists in the scheduling of court hearings and the management of legal documents given to the judge for review.

15.10 Will there be a court reporter, and what will he or she do?

A *court reporter* is a professional trained to make an accurate record of the words spoken and documents offered into evidence during court proceedings.

A written transcript of a court proceeding may be purchased from the court reporter. If your case is appealed, the transcript prepared by the court reporter will be used by the appeals court to review the facts of your case.

The court reporter is also responsible for managing documents and other items offered into evidence at trial.

Some comments or conversations are held "off the record," which means that the court reporter is not making a record of what is being said. Ordinarily, these are matters for which no appeal is expected to be taken.

Divorce in New York

15.11 Will I be able to talk to my attorney while we are in court?

During court proceedings it is important that your attorney give his or her attention to anything being said by the judge, witnesses, or your spouse's lawyer. For this reason, your attorney will avoid talking with you when anyone else in the courtroom is speaking.

Plan to have pen and paper with you when you go to court. If your court proceeding is underway and your lawyer is listening to what is being said by others in the courtroom, write him or her a note with your questions or comments.

It is critical that your attorney hear each question asked by the other lawyer and all answers given by each witness. If not, opportunities for making objections to inappropriate evidence may be lost. You can support your attorney in doing an effective job for you by avoiding talking to him or her while a court hearing is in progress.

If your court hearing is lengthy, breaks will be taken. You can use this time to discuss with your attorney any questions or observations you have about the proceeding.

15.12 What questions might my lawyer ask me at the trial about the problems in our marriage and why I want the divorce?

Because your divorce is likely to be a "no-fault" divorce, your lawyer will ask you questions to show the court that the marriage is irretrievably broken, as required by New York law. The question will be similar to this:

Attorney: Has your marriage been irretrievably broken for more than six months before you filed this proceeding?
You: Yes.

15.13 My lawyer said that the judge has issued a *pretrial order* having to do with my upcoming trial and that we'll have to "comply" with it. What does this mean?

Ask your lawyer for a copy of the *pretrial order*. Some judges will order that certain information be provided either to the opposing party or to the judge in advance of trial. This might include:

- A *statement and proposed disposition*
- A list of issues that have been settled
- A list of issues that are still disputed
- An updated statement of net worth
- A proposed parenting plan
- Agreements, referred to as *stipulations,* as to the truth of certain facts
- Names of witnesses
- Exhibits

Deadlines are given for providing the information.

15.14 What is a *pretrial conference*?

A *pretrial conference* is a meeting held within a week or two of the first day of trial with the lawyers and the judge to review information related to an upcoming trial, such as how long the trial is expected to last, the issues in dispute, and the law surrounding the disputed issues. An exploration into the possibility of settlement occurs as well.

If a pretrial conference is held in your case, ask your attorney whether you should attend. Some judges insist on the clients attending, others don't.

15.15 Besides meeting with my lawyer, is there anything else I should do to prepare for my upcoming trial?

Yes. Be sure to review your deposition and any information you provided in your discovery, such as answers to interrogatories. At trial, it is possible that you will be asked some of the same questions. If you think you might give different answers at trial, discuss this with your lawyer. You should be familiar with virtually every document that will be put into evidence for your side of the case. Review all appraisals and expert's reports as well.

It is important that your attorney know in advance of trial whether any information you provided during the discovery process has changed.

15.16 I'm meeting with my lawyer to prepare for trial. How do I make the most of these meetings?

Meeting with your lawyer to prepare for your trial is important to achieving a good outcome. Come to the meeting prepared to discuss the following:

- The issues in your case
- Your desired outcome on each of the issues
- The questions you might be asked at trial by both lawyers
- The exhibits that will be offered into evidence during the trial
- The witnesses for your trial
- The status of negotiations

Your meeting with your lawyer will help you better understand what to expect at your trial and make the trial experience easier.

15.17 My lawyer says that the law firm is busy with "trial preparation." What exactly is my lawyer doing to prepare for my trial?

Countless tasks are necessary to perform to prepare your case for trial. These are just some of them:

- Preparing the documents required by the pretrial order or the trial readiness order
- Developing arguments to be made on each of the contested issues
- Reviewing all witness depositions and expert reports
- Researching and reviewing the relevant law in your case
- Preparing the scripts/outlines for the testimony of witnesses on your behalf
- Reviewing the facts of your case to determine which witnesses are best suited to testifying about them
- Preparing the cross-examination of the opposing side's witnesses and experts
- Reviewing, selecting, and preparing exhibits

- Preparing an opening statement
- Preparing a memorandum of law concerning any unusual issues
- Reviewing rules on evidence to prepare for any objections to be made or opposed at trial
- Determining the order of witnesses and all exhibits
- Preparing your file for the day of court, including preparing a trial notebook with essential information

Your lawyer is committed to a good outcome for you in your divorce. He or she will be engaged in many important actions to fully prepare your case for trial.

15.18 My divorce is scheduled for trial. Does this mean there is no hope for a settlement?

Many cases are settled after a trial date is set. The setting of a trial date may cause you and your spouse to think about the risks and costs of going to trial. This can help you and your spouse focus on what is most important to you and lead you toward a negotiated settlement. Because the costs of preparing for and proceeding to trial are substantial, it is best to engage in settlement negotiations well in advance of your trial date.

15.19 Can I prevent my spouse from being in the courtroom?

No. Because your spouse has a legal interest in the outcome of your divorce, he or she has a right to be present. New York courtrooms are open to the public, and it is not uncommon even for persons uninvolved in your divorce to pass through the courtroom at various times simply because they have other business with the court.

15.20 Can I take a friend or family member with me to court?

Yes. Let your attorney know in advance if you intend to bring anyone to court with you. Some people important to you may be very emotional about your divorce or your spouse. Be sure to invite only someone who is better able to focus attention on supporting you rather than on his or her own feelings.

15.21 Can my friends and family be present in the courtroom during my trial?

It depends upon whether they will be witnesses in your case. In most cases in which witnesses other than the husband and wife are testifying, the attorneys request that the judge exclude all witnesses from the courtroom unless they are testifying. Once a witness has completed his or her testimony, he or she will ordinarily be allowed to remain in the courtroom for the remainder of the trial.

15.22 I want to do a great job testifying as a witness in my divorce trial. What are some tips?

To be a good witness on your own behalf, keep the following in mind: Tell the truth. Although this may not always be comfortable, it is critical if you want your testimony to be believed by the judge.

- Listen carefully to the complete question before considering your answer.

- Slow down. It's easy to speed up our speech when we are anxious. Taking your time with your answers ensures that the judge hears you and that the court reporter can accurately record your testimony.

- If you don't understand a question or don't know the answer, be sure to say so.

- If the question calls for a "yes" or "no" answer, simply state that. Then wait for the attorney to ask you the next question. If there is more you want to explain, remember that you have already told your attorney all of the important facts and he or she will make sure you are allowed to give any testimony significant in your case.

- Don't argue with the judge or the lawyers.

- Take your time. You may be asked some questions that call for a thoughtful response. If you need a moment to reflect on an answer before you give it, allow yourself that time.

- Stop speaking if an objection is made by one of the lawyers. Wait until the judge has decided whether to allow you to answer.

15.23 Should I be worried about being cross-examined by my spouse's lawyer at trial?

If your case goes to trial, prepare to be asked some questions by your spouse's lawyer. Many of these questions will call for a simple "yes" or "no."

If you are worried about particular questions, discuss your concerns with your attorney. He or she can support you in giving a truthful response. Focus on preparing well for being asked questions by your spouse's lawyer. Try not to take the questions personally; the opposing lawyer is fulfilling a duty to advocate for your spouse's interests. Remember that you are just doing your best to tell the truth about the facts.

15.24 What happens on the day of trial?

Although no two trials are alike, the following steps will occur in most divorce trials:

- Attorneys meet with the judge in chambers to discuss procedural issues, such as how many witnesses will be called, how long the case will take to present, and when breaks might be taken.

- A last-ditch effort to settle may occur.

- Attorneys give opening statements.

- Plaintiff's attorney calls plaintiff's witnesses to testify. Defendant's attorney may cross-examine each of them.

- Defendant's attorney calls defendant's witnesses to testify. Plaintiff's attorney may cross-examine each of them.

- Plaintiff's lawyer calls any rebuttal witnesses, that is, witnesses whose testimony contradicts the testimony of the defendant's witnesses.

- If there are expert witnesses needed to testify, they may be taken "out of turn" due to the fact that their availability may be limited, and they can be expensive.

- Closing arguments are made first by plaintiff's attorney and then by defendant's attorney.

15.25 Will the judge decide my case the day I go to court?

Probably not. Often there is so much information from the trial for the judge to consider that it is not possible for the judge to give an immediate ruling.

The judge may want to review documents, review the law, perform calculations, review his or her notes, and give thoughtful consideration to the issues to be decided. For this reason, it may be days, weeks, or in some cases, even longer before a ruling is made.

The judge may ask the lawyers to submit posttrial memos arguing the merits of their positions by making reference to particular portions of the transcript.

16

The Appeals Process

You may find that despite your best efforts to settle your case, your divorce went to trial and the judge made major decisions that you think will have a serious negative impact on your future. You may be either gravely disappointed or even shocked by the judge's ruling.

The judge might have seen your case differently than you and your attorney did. Perhaps the judge made mistakes. Or it may be that New York law simply does not allow for the outcome you were hoping for.

Whatever the reasons for the court's rulings, you may feel that the judge's decisions are not ones that you can live with. If this is the case, talk to your lawyer immediately about your right to appeal. Together you can decide whether an appeal is in your best interests, or whether it is better to accept the court's ruling and invest your energy in moving forward with your future without an appeal.

16.1 How much time after my divorce do I have to file an appeal?

You must file a notice of appeal within thirty days of the day your attorney is served with the decision/order with notice of entry. Because your attorney may also recommend filing certain motions following your trial, discuss how these motions may affect your appeal rights and deadlines with your lawyer as soon as you have received the judge's ruling.

A timely discussion with your attorney about your right to appeal is essential so important deadlines are not missed.

16.2 What parts of the judgment of divorce can be appealed?

If you or your spouse is unhappy with the final decisions made by the judge in your case, either of you can file an appeal. Decisions that can be appealed include custody, parenting time, child support, maintenance, distribution of property, and counsel fee awards.

16.3 Will my attorney recommend I appeal specific aspects of the decree or will I need to make a request?

Your attorney may counsel you to file an appeal on certain issues of your case; you may also ask your lawyer whether there is a legitimate basis for an appeal of any decision you believe is wrong. Talk to your attorney regarding the decisions most dissatisfying to you. Your lawyer can advise which issues have the greatest likelihood of success on appeal, in light of the facts of your case and New York law.

16.4 Can I appeal a *pendente lite* order?

Yes, but the prospects of winning the appeal are slim. The appeals court often denies the appeal and says that your remedy for any perceived inadequacies is a speedy trial.

16.5 When should an appeal be filed?

Appeals are time consuming and costly. An appeal should be filed only after careful consultation with your lawyer when you believe that the judge has made a serious error under the law or the facts of your case. Among the factors you and your attorney should discuss are:

- Whether the judge had authority under the law to make the decisions set forth in your decree
- The likelihood of the success of your appeal
- The risk that an appeal by you will encourage an appeal by your former spouse
- The cost of an appeal
- The length of time an appeal can be expected to take
- The impact of a delay in the case during the appeal

16.6   Are there any disadvantages to filing an appeal?

There can be disadvantages to filing an appeal, including:

- Uncertainty in the outcome
- Increased attorneys fees and costs
- The risk of a worse outcome on appeal than you received at trial—you could "win" the appeal only to have the issue you "won" sent back to the trial judge to have it tried again.
- Delay
- Prolonged conflict between you and your former spouse
- The risk of a second trial occurring after the appeal
- Difficulty in obtaining closure and moving forward with your life

16.7   Is an attorney necessary to appeal?

Technically, no. You can try and do it yourself, but the appeal process is very detailed and specific, with set deadlines and specific court rules. Given the complex nature of the appellate process, you should have an attorney if you intend to file an appeal.

16.8   How long does the appeals process usually take?

It depends. An appeal can take anywhere from several months to well over a year. An appeal may also result in the appellate court requiring further proceedings by the trial court. This will result in further delay.

16.9   What are the steps in the appeals process?

There are many steps that your lawyer will take on your behalf in the appeal process, including:

- Identifying the issues to be appealed
- Filing a notice with the court of your intent to appeal
- Obtaining the necessary court documents and trial exhibits to send to the appellate court

- Obtaining transcript of trial (a written copy of testimony by witnesses and statements by the judge and the lawyers made in the presence of the court reporter)
- Performing legal research to support your arguments on appeal
- Preparing and filing a document known as a "brief," which sets forth the facts of the case and the relevant law, complete with citations to court transcript, court documents, and prior cases
- Reviewing the opposing side's brief
- Preparing and filing a reply brief
- Possibly making an oral argument before the judges of the appellate court

16.10 Is filing and pursuing an appeal expensive?

Yes. In addition to filing fees and lawyer fees, there is likely to be a substantial cost for the preparation of the transcript of the trial testimony.

16.11 If I do not file an appeal, can I ever go back to court to change my decree?

Certain aspects of a decree are not modifiable, such as the division of property and debts or the award of attorney fees. Other parts of your decree, such as special support, child support, or matters regarding the children, may be modified under certain conditions.

In Closing

A s the divorce process draws to a close, you may pause and breathe. Acknowledge yourself for the courage you have shown in examining your unique situation, needs, and goals. Now you are facing your future—recasting yourself into a new life. You are looking more closely at your living situation, the needs of your children, your financial security, and your personal growth and healing. You are seeing your situation and telling the truth about what you now need. You are taking action to propel yourself into new possibilities.

It is time to take inventory of the lessons learned, goals met, and actions yet to take. Celebrate each of those steps and be gentle with yourself over the occasional misstep. You have transitioned through this difficult time when everything is reduced to the core of you. Gone are the familiar habits of your marriage. With every day moving closer to the completion of your divorce, your grief will begin to subside and your energy improve as you move toward a fresh start. All the best to you as you accomplish this life journey.

Glossary

Affidavit: A written statement of facts made under oath and signed before a notary public. Affidavits are used primarily when there will not be a hearing in open court with live testimony. The attorney will prepare an affidavit to present relevant facts. Affidavits may be signed by the parties or in some cases by witnesses. The person signing the affidavit may be referred to as the *affiant.*

Allegation: A statement that one party claims is true.

Answer: A written response to the complaint for divorce. It serves to admit or deny the allegations in the complaint and may also make claims against the opposing party. This is sometimes called a *responsive pleading.*

Appeal: The process by which a higher court reviews the decision of a lower court.

Application to modify: A party's written request to the court to change a prior order regarding custody, child support, maintenance or any other order that the court may change by law.

Child support: Financial support for a child paid by the noncustodial parent to the custodial parent.

Court order: A document setting forth the judge's orders. An order can be issued based upon the parties' agreement or the judge's decision. An order may require the parties to perform certain acts or set forth their rights and responsibilities. An order is put in writing, signed by the judge, and filed with the court.

Court order acceptable for processing (COAP): A type of court order that provides for payment of civil service retirement to a former spouse.

Complaint: The first pleading filed with the clerk of the court in an action for divorce, separation, or paternity. The complaint sets forth the facts on which the requested relief is based.

Contempt of court: The willful and intentional failure of a party to comply with a court order, judgment, or decree. Contempt may be punishable by a fine or jail.

Contested case: Any case in which the parties cannot reach an agreement. A contested case will result in a trial to have the judge decide disputed issues.

Cross-examination: The questioning of a witness by the opposing counsel during trial or at a deposition.

Custody: The legal right and responsibility awarded by a court for the possession of, care of, and decision-making for a minor child.

Defendant: The responding party to a divorce; the party who did not file the complaint initiating the divorce.

Deposition: A party or witness's testimony taken out of court, under oath, and in the presence of lawyers and a court reporter. If a person gives a different testimony at the time of trial, he or she can be impeached with the deposition testimony; that is, statements made at a deposition can be used to show untruthfulness if a different answer is given at trial.

Direct examination: The initial questioning of a witness in court by the lawyer who called him or her to testify.

Discovery: A process used by attorneys to obtain information from the opposing party for the purpose of fully assessing a case for settlement or trial. Types of discovery include interrogatories, requests for production of documents, and requests for admissions.

Equitable distribution of property: The method by which real and personal property and debts are divided in a divorce. Given all economic circumstances of the parties, New York law requires that marital property and debts be divided in a fair and reasonable manner.

Ex parte: Usually in reference to a motion, the term describes an appearance of only one party before the judge, without other party being present. For example, an *ex parte* restraining order may be granted immediately after the filing of a complaint for divorce.

Glossary

Guardian *ad litem* (GAL): A person, often a lawyer or mental health professional, appointed by court to conduct an investigation regarding the children's best interests.

Hearing: Any proceeding before the court for the purpose of resolving disputed issues between the parties through presentation of testimony, affidavits, exhibits, or argument.

Hold-harmless clause: A term in a court order or agreement that requires one party to assume responsibility for a debt and to protect the other spouse from any loss or expense in connection with it, as in to hold harmless from liability.

Interrogatories: Written questions sent from one party to the other that are used to obtain facts or opinions related to the divorce.

Joint legal custody: The shared right and responsibility of parents awarded by the court for mutual decision-making for children.

Joint physical custody: The shared right and responsibility of the parents for possession and care of a minor child.

Judgment of divorce: A final court order dissolving the marriage, dividing property and debts, ordering support, and entering other orders regarding finances and the minor children.

Maintenance: Spousal support payments from one party to another, often to enable the recipient spouse to become economically independent.

Mediation: A process by which a neutral third party facilitates negotiations between the parties on a wide range of issues.

Motion: A written application to the court for relief, such as temporary child support, custody, or restraining orders.

No fault divorce: The type of divorce that does not require evidence of marital misconduct. This means that abandonment, cruelty, and adultery are neither relevant nor required to be proven for the purposes of granting the divorce.

Notice of hearing: A written statement sent to the opposing lawyer or spouse listing the date and place of a hearing and the nature of the matters that will be heard by the court. In New York, one party is required to give the other party reasonable notice of any court hearing.

Party: The person in a legal action whose rights or interests will be affected by the divorce. For example, in a divorce the parties include the wife and husband.

Pending: During the case. For example, the judge may award you temporary support while your case is pending.

Petitioner: A term formerly used to refer to the plaintiff or person who files the complaint seeking a divorce.

Plaintiff: The person who files the complaint initiating a divorce.

Pleadings: Documents filed with the court containing factual statements which request a final judgment.

Qualified domestic relations order (QDRO): A type of court order that provides for direct payment from a qualified retirement account to a former spouse.

Qualified medical support order (QMSO): A type of court order that provides a former spouse certain rights regarding medical insurance and information.

Request for production of documents: A written request for documents sent from one party to the other during the discovery process.

Sequester: To order prospective witnesses out of the courtroom until they have concluded giving their testimony.

Set off: A debt or financial obligation of one spouse that is deducted from the debt or financial obligation of the other spouse.

Settlement: The agreed resolution of disputed issues.

Stipulation: An agreement reached between parties or an agreement by their attorneys.

Subpoena: A document delivered to a person or witness that requires him or her to appear in court, appear for a deposition, or produce documents. Failure to comply could result in punishment by the court. A subpoena requesting documents is called a subpoena *duces tecum.*

Temporary restraining order (TRO): An order of the court prohibiting a party from certain behavior. For example, a temporary restraining order may order a person not to transfer any funds during a pending divorce action.

Trial: A formal court hearing in which the judge will decide disputed issues raised by the parties' pleadings.

Under advisement: A term used to describe the status of a case, usually after a court hearing on a motion or a trial, when the judge has not yet made a decision.

Index

Index

paying, 43–44
reimbursement for, 150
written fee agreement for, 44
automatic orders, 13, 77, 124, 147
automatic stay, 151

B

bad-mouthing your spouse, 27
bank accounts
  division of, 127, 133
  emptying of, 76–77
  value of, 131
bankruptcy, 150–151
bankruptcy attorney, 151
behavior, 25, 76, 83
beneficiary, 143–144
benefits, 139–145
  employment, 139, see also retirement benefits
  health insurance, 32, 139–140
  life insurance, 144
  military, 144–145
  pension, 139–143
  retirement, 139
  Social Security, 144
  survivorship, 143
  taxes and, 152
bonuses, 108
buying sprees, 113

C

capital gains taxes, 155, 156
childcare expenses, 113–114
childcare tax credit, 157
child/children, 24, 82–83, see also child custody; child support
  abduction of, 77
  anxiety of, 25, 36, 68
  attorney for, 34–35
  best interests of, 82, 95, 101
  counseling for, 24

as dependents, 156–157
impact of divorce on, 80
initial conference/consultation, attendance to, 36
mediation and negotiation, benefits to, 66, 68
positive relationships with, 27–28
relocation of, 77–78
safety of, 83, 96
child custody, 80–104, *see also* parenting time
  abandonment and, 90
  abuse and, 97
  affair, impact on, 88–89
  age of child, impact on, 82
  attorney's role in, 92
  basis for awarding, 82–83
child's preferences for, 84–85, 92
child support and, calculating of, 108
communication about, 99
court order for, 77, 84
  dating and, 89–90
  death and, 103–104
  denial of, 93–94, 102
  domestic violence and, 97–98
  emotional ties with parents and, 82
  forensic evaluator's role in, 93
  gender of child and determining, 82
  guardian *ad litem* for, 92–93, 96
  joint, 94–95
  live-in partner and chances of getting, 87–88
  modification of, 157
  parenting plan for, 95–96
  parenting time, refusal to go

to, 102–103
pendente lite order for, 84
temporary order for, 84, 106
therapy and chances of getting, 87
types of, 80–81, 95, 103
video of daily routines for, 93
visitation and, 84, 87
witnesses role in receiving, 90–92
child support, 105–115, 177
from adoptive parent, 111
application for, 42
buying sprees as substitution for, 113
calculating, 107–109, 113, 116
child care expenses and, 113–114
contempt of court for failure to pay, 113
court order for, 11, 112, 114
date for receipt of, 110–111
determining which parent receives, 116
direct payments of, 110
for education, 114–115
future income and, 128
home equity and, 124
income attachment for additional, 111
income taxes on, 153
interest on past-due, 112
laws for, 105
length of time for receiving, 112
modification of, 157, 174
from non-biological parent, 111
partner, impact on receiving, 112
payments for, 107, 110, 112–113

pendente lite order for, 107
recipient of, factors in determining, 105, 148
relocation and, 112
remarriage and, 112
requesting, 106
during summer vacation, 111
Support Collection Services for obtaining, 109–110
temporary, 106–107
Child Support Standards Act (CSSA), 105, 107
civil restraining order, 75, *see also* restraining orders
closure, 66
COBRA, 140
collaborative divorce, 63
collaborative law, 63
college, 114–115
communication
about attorney's fees, 46
about child custody, 99
with attorney, 5–6, 27, 31
avoiding, 49
during mediation and negotiation, 65–66
types of, 37
community property, 123
complaint, 15, 57, 178, *see also* divorce complaint
compliance, 69, 103
conference, *see* initial conference/consultation
confidential information, 23
conflicts of interest, 20
consultation, *see* initial conference/consultation
contempt of court, 113, 122, 128, 178
contested court, 178
continuances, 162
cost-of-living allowance (COLA), 142

Index

Index

Index

liquid assets, 127
live-in partner, 87–88
local bar association programs, 41

M

maintenance support, 179, *see* spousal support
marital assets, *see also* assets; property division; specific types of
comingling, 129–130
division of, 123
retirement benefits as, 139
selling of, 76–77
marital debt, 146, 149, *see also* debt
marital property, 123, *see also* property division
marital status, 155
marriage, 7–8, 26
married filing a joint return filing status, 155
married filing a separate return filing status, 155
Martindale-Hubbell and Best Lawyers in America, 4
mediation and negotiation, 60–72, 179
agreements for, 20, 62, 65, 67, 69, 71
anxiety during, 68
attorney's role in, 68–71
benefits of, 64–66
boundaries of, 60
for children as dependents, 156
children attending, 68
collaborative divorce, differentiating from, 63
definition of, 62
delays in divorce resulting from, 64
differentiating between, 62–63

failure of, 69
fees for, 69
for home equity, 124
lawsuit following, 62
length of time for, 63–64
prenuptial agreements and, 136–137
preparing, 68
process for, 63–64
proposal during, asking for, 61–62
requirement for, 67
for settlement, 62
with support professionals, 66
for taxes, 152
trial, prior to, 66
types of issues for, 67–68
mediators, 62–64, 67
medical records, 102
medical treatment, 102
mental health forensic expert, 35, 45–46, 96
mental health records, 87
military benefits, 144–145
miscellaneous deductions for taxes, 157
moral fitness of parent, 82
mortgage refinancing, 125, 150
motions, 15–16, 55, 106–107, 179

N

name change, 21
negotiation, *see* mediation and negotiation
negotiation conversation, 60
New York State Law Review Commission, 128
New York State Unified Court System, 13
no-fault divorce, 7–8, 164, 179
non-biological parent, child support from, 111

189

Index

pretrial order, 164–165
primary care provider, 85–87,
  102
primary physical custody, 95
prior divorce, 35
private school, 114
privileged information, 23, 57,
  74
professional advice, 31
property, 123, *see also* property
  division
  inventory of, 126–127
  out-of-state, 128
  personal, 126
  valuation of, 131–132
property division, 123–138,
  178, *see also* property
  settlement
  of assets, 129, 135
  death, impact on, 138
  of debt, 138
  determining, 123–124
  of embryo and sperm rights,
  138
  of engagement ring, 129
  of financial accounts, 133
  of future income, 128–129
  get for, obtaining of, 138
  of gifts, 130–131
  of home equity, 124–125
  of household goods/
  furnishings, 126
  of inheritances, 130–131
  of interests and dividends,
  133
  inventory of, 126–127
  of joint business, 134–135
  judge's role in determining,
  131
  of liquid assets, 127
  modification of, 174
  pet custody and, 127–128
  prenuptial agreement for,
  136–137

stipulation of settlement for,
  131
  of stock, 135–136
  for taxes, 152
  valuation of, 131–132
property settlement, 131–133
  income taxes and, 152
  pension plan, impact on, 142
  prenuptial agreement and,
  136
  purpose of, 121
  property transfers, 152
  proposal, asking for, 61–62
  pro se, 2
  protection order, 74–76
  psychiatrist, 35, 93
  psychologist, 35, 93
  public knowledge of divorce,
  14

Q

Qualified Domestic Relations
  Order (QDRO), 143, 180
Qualified Medical Support
  Order (QMSO), 140, 180

R

reconciliation, 26–27
recused judge, 20
refinancing mortgage, 125,
  150
reimbursement, 150
religious barriers, removal of,
  138
relocation, 77–78, 100–101,
  112, 121
remarriage, 112, 121
residency requirements, 8,
  10–11, 106
responsive pleading, 177
restraining orders, 75–76, 178,
  180
retainer agreements, 40–41,
  44, 47
retainer fees, 40–41, 44, 47
retirement benefits, 14, 32,

Index

About the Author

Michael D. Stutman is president of the American Academy of Matrimonial Lawyers, New York Chapter, and is a partner and head of the Family Group of Mishcon de Reya New York, LLP (www.mishconnewyork.com), part of the international law firm Mishcon de Reya. He is the president of the American Academy of Matrimonial Lawyers, New York Chapter. He has more than thirty years of family law experience, handling all forms of nuptial agreement, divorce, settlements, and court trials.

Michael is a fellow of the International Academy of Matrimonial Lawyers and belongs to the City Bar Association and the New York State Bar Association. He served on the Committee on Matrimonial Law of the City Bar Association from 1996 to 1999 and again from 2005 to 2008. He served on the City Bar Association Committee on Trusts, Estates, and Surrogates Courts from 2008 to 2011 and is currently serving on that committee through 2015.

Michael received a Commitment to Justice Award, 1999-2000, from inMotion Online, formerly the Network for Women's Services. He has been included in "Best Lawyers in America" every year since 2007 and has been selected as a "Super

Lawyer" since that ranking was established. Michael is rated AV by Martindale-Hubbell.

Michael has frequently chaired Continuing Legal Education (CLE) programs sponsored by the City Bar Association, New York State Bar Association, and AAML-NY Chapter. He is a frequent panelist at New York State Bar Association and AAML CLE programs. Most recently he was featured as a speaker at the 2012 New York State Bar Annual Meeting of Trusts and Estates Section on Recent Changes of NY Matrimonial Law and at the 2012 Divorce Conference AICPA/AAML in Las Vegas where he spoke about "Active Passive Valuation Issues" and "Assessing Post Judgment Third Party Clawbacks and the Impact of Valuation."

He lives on the lower east side of Manhattan with his wife and their two children.

Divorce Titles from Addicus Books
Visit our online catalog at www.AddicusBooks.com